American Architecture Since 1780 A Guide to the Styles

American Architecture Since 1780 A Guide to the Styles

Marcus Whiffen

The M.I.T. Press
Massachusetts Institute of Technology
Cambridge, Massachusetts
and London, England

Ninth printing, 1985
First MIT Press paperback edition, 1981
Copyright © 1969 by
The Massachusetts Institute of Technology
All rights reserved. No part of this book may be reproduced or utilized in any form or by any means, electronic or mechanical, including photocopying, recording, or by any information storage and retrieval system, without permission in writing from the publisher.

Set in Fototronic Zenith by Graphic Services, Inc.
Printed and bound in the United States of America by Halliday Lithograph
Designed by Gerald Cinamon.

Library of Congress catalog card number: 69-10376
ISBN 0-262-23034-8 (hard)
    0-262-73057-X (paper)

To my students in AC 301
1961-1967

Preface

Two circumstances combined to give the author the idea of this book. One was that for several years his professional duties had included the teaching of a course in the history of American architecture to classes of undergraduate students whose major fields of study were seldom history and never architecture; the other was that for many more years the occupations of his leisure had included bird watching. It was this second circumstance that led to the presence in his car, as he was driving to class one morning, of Roger Tory Peterson's *Field Guide to the Western Birds,* and it was the presence in his car at that time of that most exemplary of bird watchers' handbooks that gave rise to the thought, "Could one not do for American architecture what Peterson has done for American birds?"

The answer, as I soon came to see, is "No." It is not possible because nature and art are not amenable to the same method of classification. The bird watcher's expertise lies in the identification of *species,* and as a rule there is little enough variation between individuals of the same species for a couple of drawings (one for each of the sexes) to suffice him as an aid. The expertise of the building watcher, so to call him, lies in the recognition of *styles,* and a style is far from being the same thing as a species. Not only may individual buildings classifiable as of the same style differ from each other in more noticeable ways than they resemble each other, but styles possess an almost limitless capacity for hybridization. Then architectural taxonomy is still in its pre-Linnaean phase, so to speak; there is no general agreement about nomenclature, and there are many trends in the architecture of the past and present that might be dignified as styles but have not been named at all. Furthermore, many writers on architecture make no distinction corresponding to that between genera and species in the classification of birds; they write of the Gothic Style and the Perpendicular Style, of the Baroque Style and the Borrominesque Style, of the Neo-Classical Style and the Adam Style, in each case using the same term, style, for the larger group and the smaller group, for the whole and one of its parts, indifferently.

Any attempt to remedy the deficiencies of architectural taxonomy would be inappropriate in a book whose whole purpose is to help the building watcher increase his knowledge of the architecture around him. In particular, any extensive use of new or little used names for the styles could lead only to confusion and frustration when he turned to other books; it proved impossible to avoid these altogether, but they have been kept to a minimum and used only when a current name seemed altogether misleading (for example, Western Stick Style instead of Bay Region Style) or when it seemed more descriptive of another style (for example, New Formalism instead of Neo-Classical Revival). It has often been necessary to choose between different names for the same style; in such cases I have usually given the reason for my choice.

The building watcher, who by definition is not an architect, should know that among architects style was "a word of bad odor" (in Suzanne Langer's phrase) in the recent past. Between 1930 and 1960, dislike of the word style, together with a refusal to recognize the realities that it stands for, united the adherents of the two extremes of architectural opinion – the romantics, who believed that an architectural design should be the product of the architect's unaided genius, and the rationalists, who believed that it should be the product of a quasi-mathematical assessment of the functions of the projected building. The fact that historians of architecture continued to employ the word was another mark against it, and them; some architects went so far as to regard the historians as necrophilous disturbers of the graveyards of the past, who might at any moment disinter a corpse whose style was still capable of infecting the living.

Things have changed in the last few years, and the five-letter word that formerly gave offense now appears with growing frequency in publications for and by architects. Some architects, though not many in America yet, have come to see that a style may be more than a convenient means of classification for the historian. Thus, for example, the Norwegian architect Christian Norberg-Schulz writes,
"The style is a cultural object on a higher level than the single work. While the individual work has one determined physical manifestation, the style has an infinite number of such manifestations. While the individual work concretizes a particular situation, the style concretizes a collection of such situations; in principle it may concretize a culture in its totality. The style therefore has a stabilizing purpose in society. It unites the individual products and makes them appear as parts of a

meaningful whole. The style furthermore preserves certain basic intentional poles and secures the cultural continuity."*

None of the styles discussed and illustrated in this book – not even the Greek Revival, despite what the late Talbot Hamlin believed – can be held to have concretized American culture in its totality. Most of them were importations that had originated elsewhere, while the collections of situations concretized by each of the indigenous styles were dominated by what was only a small part of that totality – by the genius of one man, as in the Richardsonian Romanesque for example, by a regional myth, as in the Mission Style, by a regional ideal, as in the Prairie Style, or by a general reaction against the immediate past, as in the New Formalism.

If a style concretizes a collection of situations, a new collection of situations must produce a new style. This sets temporal limits to any style – or perhaps one should say to the vitality of any style, for what began as a response to certain needs may degenerate into a mere habit of design, perpetuated by minor architects long after new needs have produced new responses. It follows that history must play a part even in the definition of a style. A Georgian Revival house of 1920 is not of the same style as a Georgian one of 1750, however accurately the details of the earlier period may be reproduced; for the same reason, certain buildings of 1900-1930 cannot simply be grouped with other buildings of 1820-1850 under the head of Greek Revival, despite their similarity of appearance and the use in them of an identical repertory of forms. While architectural styles can always be *described* in terms of the visible characteristics of the buildings in them, it is not always possible to *distinguish* them in those terms alone.

For all that, the first step in acquiring a knowledge of architecture, for anyone with a nonprofessional interest in the subject, is to learn to see those visible characteristics by looking at buildings. Subsequent steps certainly should take him over the thresholds of those buildings whenever possible. If it is not often possible, there is no dishonor, and there can be much pleasure, in remaining a building watcher. For that particular man in the street, whose experience of buildings is generally limited

Intentions in Architecture (Cambridge: The M.I.T. Press, 1965), pp. 157-158.

to the outside view, this book is designed. It contains no interiors and no plans, as it certainly would if it were a history or a work of criticism instead of what it is – a guide to the architectural styles as the building watcher sees them.

The photographs and the descriptive paragraphs that precede the historical sections are intended to supplement each other. The reader is asked to believe that if a photograph should show a feature not mentioned in the text, or even a feature that the text would seem to deny to the style in question, it may be due to the author's desire to spare him the endless qualifying phrases and enumeration of exceptions that a description which could not be faulted on any point would require. The captions have been separated from the photographs for a set purpose: to help the user of the book get a composite picture of the style before letting his attention become distracted by questions of identity, location, architect, or date. There is a glossary to diminish the need to refer to other books, and there is a bibliography to facilitate reference to them. The index gives the years of the birth and death of the architects represented or mentioned, when I have been able to discover them.

Marcus Whiffen
Arizona State University
Tempe, Arizona
January 1968

Author's Acknowledgment

The assistance of the Arizona State University Faculty Grant-In-Aid Program, under which the author was awarded a grant toward the support of his work on this book, is gratefully acknowledged. It is also a pleasure to record debts of gratitude, for their generous response to appeals for information, to Bainbridge Bunting, Gordon Heck, George A. McMath, Buford Pickens, and Victor Steinbrueck.

M. W.

Contents

Preface	vii
A Note on the Colonial Styles	3
1: Styles That Reached Their Zenith in 1780-1820	**21**
The Adam Style	23
Jeffersonian Classicism	31
2: Styles That Reached Their Zenith in 1820-1860	**37**
The Greek Revival	38
The Egyptian Revival	48
The Early Gothic Revival	53
The Romanesque Revival	61
The Italian Villa Style	69
The Renaissance Revival: the Romano-Tuscan Mode	75
The Renaissance Revival: the North Italian Mode	79
The Octagon Mode	83
3: Styles That Reached Their Zenith in 1860-1890	**87**
High Victorian Gothic	89
High Victorian Italianate	97
The Second Empire Style	103
The Stick Style	109
The Queen Anne Style	115
The Eastlake Style	123
The Shingle Style	127
Richardsonian Romanesque	133
Châteauesque	141
4: Styles That Reached Their Zenith in 1890-1915	**147**
Beaux-Arts Classicism	149
The Second Renaissance Revival	154
The Georgian Revival	159
The Neo-Classical Revival	167
The Late Gothic Revival	173
The Jacobethan Revival	178
The Commercial Style	183

Sullivanesque	191
The Prairie Style	201
The Western Stick Style	209
The Mission Style	213
Bungaloid	217
5: Styles That Reached Their Zenith in 1915-1945	223
The Spanish Colonial Revival	225
The Pueblo Style	229
Modernistic	235
The International Style	241
6: Styles That Have Flourished Since 1945	249
Miesian	251
The New Formalism	257
Wrightian	263
Neo-Expressionism	269
Brutalism	275
Bibliography	281
Glossary	291
Index	301

American Architecture Since 1780 A Guide to the Styles

1. *The Old Brick Church* (*St. Luke's*), *Newport Parish, Virginia*
Built in 1632, except for the upper part of the tower, this is a unique example of Gothic Survival. (Photo: Author)

A Note on the Colonial Styles

The Old Brick Church of Newport Parish, in Isle of Wight County, Virginia, is now known to be the oldest existing English colonial building in North America. (Research undertaken in connection with its restoration twelve years ago confirmed 1632 as the date of all but the upper part of the tower.) With its heavily buttressed walls, pointed arches, and window tracery, it represents a survival of Gothic architecture into the century of the Baroque easily enough accounted for by the fact that there were as yet no churches in any more recent style in the mother country itself, where there had been little need for new churches during the preceding hundred years.

When it comes to domestic architecture in the English colonies in the seventeenth century, the epithets Gothic and Medieval should be used with more caution than some writers have exercised. It is true that construction techniques employed in the houses of the time had not

2. *Boardman House, Saugus, Massachusetts*
Representing the New England type of two-story house with central chimney and projecting upper floor, or jetty, this was built in 1686. (Photo: Author)

changed since the fifteenth century and that one usually looks in vain for classical forms that would indicate Renaissance influence. Yet in the reign of Elizabeth I there had been a tremendous improvement in the standard of housing in the English countryside. The type of house that became dominant in seventeenth-century New England, of two full stories and having a massive central chimney, was a product of this housing revolution, unknown before it, and therefore Elizabethan rather than Medieval. The dominant Southern type in the seventeenth century, and down into the nineteenth for modest dwellings, was of one story or a story and a half (that is, with dormer windows lighting rooms in the roof) with a chimney at either end. It too was of English origin; its central passage – "a passage . . . through the middle of the house for an air-draught in summer," as a writer described it in 1724 – helped ensure its survival as the fittest type in the Southern climate just as the central chimney, warming rooms on two floors on

3. *Burlington, Charles City County, Virginia*
An eighteenth-century example of the very persistent story-and-a-half Southern type. The porch is nineteenth century. (Photo: Author)

either side, established the other type in New England with its bitter winters. In ecclesiastical architecture there was a corresponding difference between New England and the South in the seventeenth century, with religion as the determining factor and buildings like the Old Ship Meeting House at Hingham, Massachusetts (built in 1681), as the Puritan counterparts of the Anglican Old Brick Church.

In seventeenth-century New Mexico the Franciscan friars, with the aid of Indian labor, tools supplied by the Spanish crown, and their own knowledge of recent European developments, were responsible in the churches of their missions for a regional architecture of extraordinary interest. At first sight such a building as San Estevan at Acoma may look crude in comparison with the practically coeval Old Brick Church. Yet far from representing, as the Virginia building does, a survival of an earlier style, San Estevan is the result of a forthright adaptation of Baroque ideas to the outlandish conditions of New Mexico. A feature

4. *San Estevan, Acoma, New Mexico*
Built (of adobe and fieldstone) between 1629 and 1644 and thus the oldest, as well as the largest, of the Spanish Colonial churches of New Mexico still in use. (HABS, Library of Congress)

5. *Westover, Charles City County, Virginia*
A handsome example of the double-pile house in its Georgian Colonial form, built in the 1730's for the rich and cultured planter William Byrd III. (Photo: Author)

6. *Miles Brewton House, Charleston, South Carolina*
With its tall proportions and two-story portico, this shows Georgian Colonial at its most Palladian. It was built in 1765-1769. (Photo: Author)

that is apparently peculiar to this architecture is the transverse clerestory window – that is, a window, transverse to the long axis of the church, between the roof of the nave and the higher roof of the sanctuary. Destroyed when the roof was altered at Acoma but still existing in several other churches of the region, the transverse clerestory window, invisible to worshipers in the nave but flooding the sanctuary and altar with light, proclaims these buildings country cousins of the great Baroque churches of seventeenth-century Rome.

It would appear that no seventeenth-century house in the English colonies, with the possible exception of the Foster-Hutchinson House in Boston (circa 1688), was more than one room deep under the main roof, though additional back rooms were often accommodated under a lean-to, or shed roof. The "double-pile" house – two rooms deep, squarish in plan, of two or two-and-a-half stories and five (or more rarely seven) sashed windows wide – appeared early in the eighteenth century and persisted, as the commonest type for houses of any consequence, down to the Revolution and beyond. It was a type that, having crystallized in England in the third quarter of the seventeenth century, was in a sense traditional by the time it crossed the Atlantic. After 1730, Georgian Colonial architecture becomes more bookish – not to dignify the development by calling it academic – as the result of the use of the builders' handbooks and architectural design books of other kinds that were being put out in considerable numbers by the London publishers. At first only individual features and interior design were affected. Examples are the doorways on the two fronts at Westover (after 1730) and the interior paneling at Carter's Grove, Virginia (1750-1753), all based on plates in William Salmon's *Palladio Londinensis*. The feature most characteristic of the domestic style of the North Italian sixteenth-century architect whose name Salmon borrowed – it having become a name to conjure with since Lord Burlington and Colen Campbell had set English architecture on a Palladian course in the 1720's – was the pedimented portico of one or two stories. The two-story form was preferred in the colonies, appearing first (it would seem) at Drayton Hall, near Charleston, South Carolina (1738-1742).

In the twenty years before the Revolution, not merely features but also whole designs for buildings were taken from books. Notable examples are the Brick Market at Newport, Rhode Island (1761), and

7. *Dalton House, Newburyport, Massachusetts*
A large town house, dating from about 1775 and illustrating the final phase of Georgian Colonial architecture before the advent of the Adam Style. (Photo: Author)

8. *St. Michael's, Charleston, South Carolina*
The unknown architect of this grand town church, built in 1752-1761, combined steeple and portico in the way popularized by James Gibbs. (Photo: Author)

9. *Christ Church, Lancaster County, Virginia*
A steepleless country church of cruciform plan, built in 1732. The tabernacle frames around the doors are of bricks cut to shape and laid with extra-fine mortar joints. (Photo: Author)

Mount Airy in Virginia (1758-1762); the façades of the former follow a published design that was believed to be by the seventeenth-century English architect Inigo Jones, who as the first to introduce the Palladian style into England was admired as much as Palladio himself by the eighteenth-century English, while Mount Airy combines two house designs in *A Book of Architecture* by James Gibbs (published in 1728). It was in church architecture that the influence of Gibbs was strongest. A new type of Anglican church building, with a galleried interior and

10. *Bries House, East Greenbush, New York*
The steep straight-sided gables with their crowning chimneys are characteristic of houses built by the Dutch. This one was built in 1723. (HABS, Library of Congress)

a steeple that achieved Gothic verticality despite the use of round arches and the classical orders, had been invented by Sir Christopher Wren after the Great Fire of London of 1666. (Old North in Boston, Massachusetts, and Trinity at Newport, Rhode Island, both built in the 1720's, are colonial examples of the Wren-type church.) Gibbs, in the church of St. Martin-in-the-Fields, which was built in 1722-1726 and stands off the northeast corner of Trafalgar Square, placed the steeple behind a pedimented portico with freestanding columns. Although critics have often expressed doubts about this arrangement, it was borrowed from Gibbs by the architects of churches all over the English-speaking world, the loan being facilitated by the plates of St. Martin's in *A Book of Architecture*. St. Michael's, Charleston, South Carolina, supplies a Georgian Colonial example. More frequently in the colonies close imitations of the steeple of St. Martin-in-the-Fields were built without porticoes, which were notoriously expensive features; a case in point is Christ Church, Philadelphia, whose steeple was completed in 1754. In the thinly populated rural parishes of the South, where church bells would never have been audible to more than a small minority of the parishioners, steepleless churches were the rule. Christ Church, Lancaster County, Virginia, is perhaps the most handsome of them.

From old views we know that the Dutch in New Amsterdam (from 1664, New York) did their best to create a home from home with tall narrow houses presenting crow-stepped gables to the street. None of them has survived, and "Dutch Colonial" is now represented by buildings dating from the eighteenth century and the early years of the nineteenth. Of houses there are two main types. One has a steep double-pitch roof with eaves to back and front only and a straight-sided gable, crowned by a chimney, at each end; the other is characterized by a very broad gambrel roof with flared eaves to the lower slopes. The Ackerman House at Hackensack, New Jersey, is a good (and early) specimen of the latter type, whose origin is still a matter of dispute; it did not come from Holland, and the theory that Protestant refugees brought it from Flanders has recently been under attack. The Middle Colonies, with Swedes and Rhinelanders in Pennsylvania, Delaware, and western New Jersey, as well as the Dutch in eastern New Jersey and New York, were a cultural melting pot as New England and the South were not,

14 A Note on the Colonial Styles

and their architecture showed this in a number of regional idiosyncrasies. Among the latter is the Pennsylvanian fondness for the pent roof. This was a feature of the London house in the seventeenth century that fire regulations had put an end to in that city; its frequent use and late survival in Pennsylvania is doubtless due to German influence.

An exception to the rule that settlers in a new land do their best to reproduce the houses of their home countries is seen in the houses built by the French in the Mississippi Valley. The type represented by

11. *Ackerman House, Hackensack, New Jersey*
This represents another well-defined type of Dutch Colonial house, with a form of gambrel roof that is peculiar to it. It dates from 1704. (HABS, Library of Congress)

the Louisiana plantation house of the eighteenth and early nineteenth centuries and (on a smaller scale) the "raised cottage" of New Orleans is not to be found in France. It may be that the West Indies contributed the full-length porch or *galerie* (what the English called the piazza). Whatever its pedigree, with the main rooms insulated from the damp earth by a full-height ground story and from the sun above by the ample hipped roof, which extends over the *galerie* to provide cool and dry outdoor space, and ventilated by tall French windows, the type was a splendid solution of the special problems posed by the climate

12. *Green Tree Inn (Pastorius House), Germantown, Pennsylvania*
Built in 1748, this has the pent roofs that remained in common use in Pennsylvania long after they had been outlawed, as an antifire measure, in London. (Photo: Author)

16 A Note on the Colonial Styles

13. *Home Place, St. Charles Parish, Louisiana*
A typical Louisiana plantation house, built in 1801, with high hipped roof, *galerie*, and outside stair leading to the main rooms on the upper floor. (Library of Congress. Photo: Frances Benjamin Johnston)

and geography of the region. During the century 1730-1830, it underwent only minor change; Home Place, illustrated here, could well have been built in 1750 rather than 1801, the actual year of its construction. From the mating of this long-established type with the Greek Revival came houses of the distinctive "peripteral mode," noted and illustrated later in these pages.

In New Mexico the seventeenth-century style continued unchanged through the eighteenth. The architecture of the other Spanish mission fields in the eighteenth century should be seen in relation to developments further to the south. The one work that does not suffer in the

14. *San José de Aguayo, near San Antonio, Texas*
This façade, carved by Pedro Huizar in 1768-1777, is with its Rococo ornament a fine example of the last phase of the Mexican Baroque. (Photo: Author)

15. *San Xavier del Bac, near Tucson, Arizona*
Although later in date than the façade of San José de Aguayo, having been built in 1783-1797, this church is earlier in style. The architect is not known. (Photo: Author)

resultant comparisons is the façade of the church of San José de Aguayo, near San Antonio, Texas; carved by Pedro Huizar between 1768 and 1777, this is as fine an example of the last, near-Rococo phase of the Mexican Baroque as can easily be found in Mexico itself. San Xavier del Bac, near Tucson, Arizona, is a surprisingly ambitious and elaborate building for what was so remote a place; yet in 1783-1797 it could hardly have been built in a place less remote, so *retardataire* was it in style. As for the mission churches of California, although they too were post-Baroque in date, only one of them, Santa Barbara with its naïve attempt at a temple-portico façade (1815-1820), acknowledged in any conspicuous way the existence of the Neo-Classical movement that had already given architecture on the eastern side of the continent new ideals and a new look.

1: Styles That Reached Their Zenith in 1780-1820

The Adam Style, which is sometimes called the Federal Style, was dominant, except in the South where Jeffersonian Classicism ruled. Most of the buildings of the Federal Period that are not classifiable under one of these heads are early examples of the Greek or Gothic revivals or represent colonial survivals.

The Adam Style

Lightness and delicacy are the qualities that mark the Adam Style. When there is an order, the columns or pilasters are attenuated, sometimes to the point of meagerness; porticoes and porches are given a light and airy effect by the wide spacing of the slender columns. Moldings and ornament are delicate and of low relief. Ornament is of a geometrical nature, even when composed of naturalistic or seminaturalistic forms; favorite types of ornament are the circular or elliptical patera and the chain of husks (though the latter is not often seen on the outside of buildings). Windows tend to be of narrower proportions than in the Georgian Colonial, and the glazing bars are always much more slender. In general form Adam Style houses may be rectilinear and boxlike, with perhaps a semicircular porch over the front door, or they may be of a more complex geometry, with curved or octagonal projections, expressing the room shapes within, played off against the basic cube; curving steps (with light iron railings) are characteristic. Curves, both segmental and elliptical, are also used in elevations much more freely than in the other classical styles. Very typical is the doorway with a semielliptical fanlight and with sidelights flanking the door, and so is the semicircular relieving arch with a window recessed within it. Roof lines are generally quiet, and in the more sophisticated examples the roof is concealed behind a balustrade.

History: The Adam Style takes its name from three brothers who in the twenty years 1760-1780 had the biggest architectural practice in England. The eldest and most gifted was Robert Adam, whose preparation for the role he was to play in the history of architecture included a visit to Spalato (now Split, in Yugoslavia) to study the palace of the Roman Emperor Diocletian. This visit, made in the company of the French architect C.-L. Clérisseau, whom Jefferson also was to know well, resulted some years later in a folio volume, dedicated to George III, as Adam's contribution to that great enlargement of the knowledge of ancient architecture which marked the second half of the eighteenth century. Among the other important contributors were Robert Wood, with books on the cities of Roman Syria, and James Stuart and Nicholas Revett, with *The Antiquities of Athens.*

The archaeological activity of the later eighteenth century affected architectural design in several ways and at several levels. It offered new models for imitation, and although certain of them – notably the temples of Greece – were not immediately acceptable to most architects, others – such as the decorative motifs of Roman Syria – were seized upon with avidity. By showing what ancient domestic and palatial interiors had really been like, it suggested that the use inside houses of forms derived from temple architecture was a solecism. Above all, it led to the realization that ancient architecture had not been nearly so standardized as had been supposed when detailed knowledge had been confined to relatively few buildings, and those all in Italy and the South of France. Even the proportions of the orders were seen not to have been sacrosanct. "The great masters of antiquity," Robert Adam wrote, "were not so rigidly scrupulous. They varied the proportions as the general spirit of their compositions required, clearly perceiving that however necessary these rules may be to form the taste and correct the

licentiousness of the scholar, they often cramp the genius and circumscribe the ideas of the master." Such talk was only less subversive than the attractiveness of the style in which Robert Adam had drawn together and interfused the new ideas and tendencies. By 1770, in England, the Adam Style had defeated and overthrown the Palladianism that had been the ruling style of the preceding fifty years.

The first American example of the Adam Style was the ceiling in the Mount Vernon dining room, executed for Washington in 1775; that it should have been an interior feature is to be expected, since it was in interior design that the Adam Style was most obviously novel, with its substitution of "a beautiful variety of light mouldings, gracefully formed, delicately enriched and arranged with propriety and skill" (to quote Robert again) for the more massive ornamentation previously used. The first whole building in the style was The Woodlands, Philadelphia, which

went up in 1787-1789 to the design, apparently, of its owner William Hamilton. With bowed projections containing the ends of oval rooms, Palladian windows set in relieving arches, and a portico of an elongated Tuscan order flanked by empty niches in the thickness of the wall, The Woodlands remains one of the most thoroughgoing essays in the style in America. It was in 1787, also, that Charles Bulfinch designed the Massachusetts State House in Boston, although it was not built until 1795-1798. Incorporating motifs from Somerset House, London, the masterpiece of Robert Adam's archenemy Sir William Chambers, translated into Adam Style terms, this is the finest governmental building in the style. Bulfinch's Christ Church, at Lancaster, Massachusetts (1816), with its arcaded porch and simple cupola, is a handsome exception to the rule that churches of its time repeat (with the usual attenuation of the classical elements) the Gibbsian formula of columned portico and multistage steeple.

For another notable public building we may return to Philadelphia for the center section of the Pennsylvania Hospital, begun in 1794 and attributed to one David Evans, Jr. However, it is as a domestic style that one thinks of the Adam Style, and it was indeed the predominant domestic style during the whole Federal Period. It may still be studied in concentration at Salem, Massachusetts, where the woodcarver-architect Samuel McIntire set the fashion by designing a series of houses in emulation of Bulfinch's in nearby Boston. To mention a few of the most notable examples elsewhere, in Baltimore there is Homewood (1798), another house apparently designed by its owner, who was Charles Carroll, Jr.; in Washington, The Octagon (since 1899 the headquarters of the American Institute of Architects), which was designed in 1798 by William Thornton, winner of the United States Capitol competition six years before. The latter, with its variously shaped rooms inside and its combination of cube and cylinder outside, demonstrates the new freedom of planning and the quality of "movement," as Robert Adam called it. In and near Charleston, South Carolina, the Joseph Manigault House, built in 1790-1797 to the design of the amateur architect Gabriel Manigault, was scarcely begun when, in 1791, a portico modeled on that designed by Robert Adam himself for David Garrick's villa at Hampton on the Thames was added to the plantation house called Hampton, at McClellanville; a later Charlestonian example is the splendid Nathaniel

Russell House, built in the first decade of the nineteenth century with Russell Warren as architect. To the northwest of Charleston, at Augusta, Georgia, the Ware-Sibley House of 1818 provides, with its oval stair and segmental porch played off against flanking octagonal bays, another example of Adam's "movement."

Beyond the Appalachians, the Adam Style had little time to establish itself before the Greek Revival carried all before it. However, at St. Matthews, near Louisville, Kentucky, there is Ridgeway, a house of tripartite composition with segmental-arched openings and a porch of the greatest delicacy built around 1805. The Taft House in Cincinnati, Ohio, built in 1820, would more than hold its own on the eastern seaboard, and the Congregational Church at Tallmadge would at least look quite at home there.

The builder-architects did not have to rely on the Adam brothers' own *Works in Architecture,* a large and costly publication, for knowledge of the new style. It found its way into the English builders' guides, such as those of William Pain, long before Robert Adam's death, and into the American ones – Asher Benjamin's, for instance – early in the nineteenth century.

Bibliography references: 1, 6, 7, 10, 34, 56, 61, 64, 65

1. Clay Hill, Harrodsburg, Kentucky. 1812. (HABS, Library of Congress. Photo: Lester Jones)
2. Nickels-Sortwell House, Wiscasset, Maine. 1807-1812. (HABS, Library of Congress. Photo: Cervin Robinson)
3. Ware-Sibley House, Augusta, Georgia. 1818. (Library of Congress. Photo: Frances Benjamin Johnston)
4. Congregational Church, Tallmadge, Ohio. Lemuel Porter, architect, 1821. (Photo: Hedrich-Blessing)
5. Lawrason-Lafayette House, Alexandria, Virginia. Circa 1820. (Photo: J. Alexander)

Jeffersonian Classicism

The quintessential Jeffersonian building is of red brick with a white portico of the Tuscan order or of unfluted Roman Doric. (Ionic and Corinthian are much rarer.) Very often there is a semicircular window in the pediment. The effect of the portico is one of weight and massiveness (as against the lightness of an Adam Style portico). It may be the central feature of the front, or the whole building may be of temple form. In either case the plan of the building is unlikely to be of any but rectilinear outline; polygonal projections may occur, but curved ones are exceptional. The general squareness is shared by the elevations, with straight-topped windows, though there may be a semicircular fanlight over the front door. Roofs are of low, pedimental pitch, sometimes concealed by balustrades. Two distinctive types of house are classifiable as Jeffersonian. One has a two-story pedimented center with single-story wings projecting on either side. The other has a hip-roofed center with pavilions linked to it by lower sections, forming a five-part composition; the pavilions may be of temple form or may have hipped roofs.

History: Thomas Jefferson's first architectural works antedate the Revolution. They include – or so it would seem, for his responsibility for their design has never been proved beyond all doubt – two or three houses of more purely classical and Palladian inspiration than the normal Southern plantation type with its hip-roofed central block and freestanding "dependencies" on either side. Then in 1784, when he was in Paris as United States Minister to France, he was asked to supply a design for a new capitol for his native Virginia. In response, he and his associate C.-L. Clérisseau (who a quarter of a century before had been Robert Adam's companion and draftsman at Spalato) made a design in which they "took as their model" the Roman temple of Augustus known as the Maison Carrée, at Nîmes in southern France. They changed the order from Corinthian to Ionic and made certain necessary concessions to function by increasing the dimensions and introducing windows but preserved the over-all form of their model intact. Thus the Virginia State Capitol at Richmond, as completed in 1792, became a landmark in the history of Neo-Classical architecture as the first public building anywhere of pure temple form, as well as the first of those temple-form buildings that fifty years later were to be so characteristic of the American scene.

Of Jefferson's later architectural works, at least two are intrinsically superior to the Virginia Capitol. In Monticello, his own country house near Charlottesville, he adopted a generally Palladian scheme but introduced a variety of features that all tended to make it more like an ancient Roman villa, as described in the writings of Cicero and the younger Pliny, than any of Palladio's own designs had been. In the University of Virginia, with its two rows of templelike pavilions facing each other across a terraced lawn dominated by a library imitating the Roman Pantheon, he realized an entirely new concept of a university as an "academical village."

Jefferson had a poor opinion of the Georgian Colonial architecture of his youth. This was not, as is sometimes supposed, because it was English. It was because it seemed to him crude and, by classical criteria,

3

illiterate; "scarcely a workman was to be found," he complained, "capable of drawing an order." For him, the Roman orders were the fundamental discipline of architectural design. Inside Monticello all three of the principal orders, Doric, Ionic, and Corinthian, are employed; at the University of Virginia each pavilion (with one exception, designed not by Jefferson but by Latrobe) displays a different version of one of them, patterned after an ancient Roman building or a plate in Palladio's treatise. He nowhere in any of his works, however, used a Greek order. He was, it has been said, the "most Roman of the Romanists" at a time when more and more architects were turning to Greece.

Jefferson's avoidance of Greek forms, surprising at first in so widely and deeply read a Hellenist, was not due to ignorance; his library contained the standard works on Greek architecture. Several circumstances combined to cause it. One whose importance should not be minimized, since direct visual experience counts for so much in any architect's development, was the fact that Jefferson had actually seen Roman buildings, in the South of France; the Maison Carrée, by his own account, had overwhelmed him. He had seen no Greek buildings at all. Then there was the consideration that the early American republic presented more analogies with the Roman Republic and early Empire than with the city states of Greece. Jefferson had read in Palladio that "Ancient architecture gives us a certain idea of Roman virtue and greatness." Might not imitations of it, by keeping the example of Rome in view, inspire Americans to emulate that virtue and greatness? In addition, Roman architecture, embracing so much wider a range of building types than Greek architecture – indeed, a wider range of building types than any architecture before Jefferson's own time – must have seemed to offer better, because more adaptable, means of providing for the varied needs of a modern nation. At the same time he rejected the Adam Style; not only did he eschew the rich ornament of the Eastern Roman Empire but inside Monticello he employed the massive entablatures that Robert Adam had listed among those interior features which thanks to his lead had been "universally exploded."

Jeffersonian Classicism was born in Virginia, and it remained a Southern style – which is not to say that it was not carried west (for example, the Kintner-Withers House, near Laconia, Indiana, 1837). It is sometimes

5

called the Roman Revival, but its character owes so much to Jefferson's personal example and influence, if only because the other architects working in it were not major talents, that it should surely bear his name.

Bibliography references: 1, 7, 10, 12, 20, 25, 35, 36, 67

1. Pavilion VII, University of Virginia, Charlottesville, Virginia. Thomas Jefferson, architect, 1817. (Photo: Author)
2. Lunenburg County Courthouse, Virginia. 1824-1827. (Photo: Author)
3. Estouteville, Albemarle County, Virginia. James Dinsmore, architect and builder, 1827. (Photo: Author)
4. Battersea, Petersburg, Virginia. Attributed to Thomas Jefferson, circa 1780; windows altered. (Photo: Author)
5. Fortsville, Southampton County, Virginia. Circa 1800; porch later. (Photo: Author)

2: Styles That Reached Their Zenith in 1820-1860

The number of going styles increased considerably during this period, which also saw the adoption of the principles of the Picturesque. Many architects worked in several styles, choosing for the job in hand whichever seemed the most appropriate for practical or symbolic reasons; until 1850, at least, Greek was the most frequent choice.

The Greek Revival

When there is an order, that is the first thing to look at. The Greek Doric is easily distinguished from the Roman Doric, for the shafts of the columns stand on the supporting surface without any molded base. The Greek Ionic in most of its versions has a capital with larger and more boldly formed volutes than Roman Ionic capitals or their Renaissance derivatives. A Greek Corinthian is less easily told from a Roman, unless it should be of the order of the Monument of Lysicrates, with palm leaves around the capital *below* the acanthus leaves, or of the Tower of the Winds, with palm leaves *above* the acanthus.

Order or no order, bilateral symmetry is the rule. The exceptions are houses, in which an L-form plan might be used for convenience' sake. Buildings are either simple rectangular blocks, without either projections or re-entrant angles, or compositions of such blocks set against each other without any transitional features. The classical temple form, with a portico across the entire front and the roof ridge running from front to back, is employed for buildings of all kinds. Wall surfaces are as smooth as the material allows. Roofs are of low pitch, like temple roofs, or flat; in the latter case there may be a solid parapet or attic over the cornice but not (unless the architect forgot himself) a balustrade. Dormers are rare because roofs are usually too low to provide habitable space and also because they spoil the temple effect; rooms in the top story are sometimes lit by windows in the frieze of the entablature crowning the walls. All windows and doors are trabeated, because the arch had no place in Greek temple architecture; the place of the Adam Style fanlight over the front door is taken by an oblong glazed opening. The commonest types of ornament are the anthemion and the Greek fret. But the smaller Greek Revival building is often without external ornament of any kind. Wooden buildings were invariably painted white.

History: The first building in the United States to incorporate a Greek order was the Bank of Pennsylvania in Philadelphia, designed by Benjamin Henry Latrobe in 1798. This had a Greek Ionic portico on either front; over the central banking hall was a low dome. Latrobe, who had come from England in 1796 to be the first professionally trained architect to work in the United States, used Greek forms in other designs, and on one occasion he wrote to his patron and friend Thomas Jefferson:

The Greek Revival

"My principles of good taste are rigid in Grecian architecture." But his work has more in common with European Neo-Classicism than with the Greek Revival in America.

The Greek Revival proper may be considered to have opened in 1818, with the competition for the design of the Second Bank of the United States in Philadelphia, in which the conditions called for "a chaste imitation of Grecian Architecture." The successful architect was William

Strickland, who had been a pupil of Latrobe. His building, best known today as the Custom House, which it became in 1844, may be seen as a "correction" of Latrobe's Bank of Pennsylvania of twenty years before. For the porticoes (which were required by the competition program) Strickland used the Doric order of the Parthenon, detailing it as accurately as he could, instead of the Ionic used by Latrobe, and he suppressed the central dome of Latrobe's bank to keep his whole building under a single temple roof. With these modifications he proclaimed his allegiance to the growing school of thought that believed in the absolute superiority of Ancient Greek architecture. For domes are Roman, not Greek, and the Greek Doric column had been the feature of Greek architecture that earlier generations of classicists had found hardest of all to stomach.

By no means all the Greek Revivalists were to follow Strickland in rejecting the dome and copying specific Greek models in their orders. Some of the best Greek Revival buildings were domed: for example, the North Carolina State Capitol at Raleigh, designed by the important firm of Town and Davis, and (as originally built) the Boston Customs House, by Ammi B. Young. As for the orders themselves, many freedoms were taken with them. A very common one was to omit the fluting from the Doric column; another was to substitute square pillars for columns. Asher Benjamin, the 1827 edition of whose book, *The American Builder's Companion,* was one of the first American handbooks to include Greek orders, pointed out that the use of a correctly proportioned Greek Doric in a house "would require the thickness of the column, at its base, to exceed the breadth of the doors and windows, and the entablature would cover one third of the front of the house." So he and others, notably Minard Lafever, set about modifying the Greek orders in the interests of practicality. The builders who used their books introduced further variations of their own, with the result that the Greek Revival cannot fairly be stigmatized as a pedantic movement, whatever its other faults.

Its weakness was its formalism, its addiction to admired forms, and one form especially, at the expense of functional considerations. As its enemy Andrew Jackson Downing put it, the "taste for Grecian temples" tended "to destroy expression of purpose." Not only was Greek architecture thought to be pre-eminently beautiful; the Greek temple was regarded as a perfect form. So buildings for all purposes were built in the form of Greek temples. Strickland maintained that the Parthenon was a very appropriate model for his bank in Philadelphia – for had not that ancient building also housed public treasure? For churches the temple form was clearly suitable, though it was usually necessary to have a steeple, and here was a difficulty because of the paucity of *vertical* models in Greek architecture, the Athenian Monument of Lysicrates (334 B.C.) and Tower of the Winds (circa 50 B.C.) being the only ones that came easily to mind. The temple form was not so obviously suited to schools and colleges, symbolically or practically. Yet it was employed for them often enough, with results ranging from simple small-town schoolhouses at one end of the scale to the fully peripteral Corinthian temple of huge dimensions into which Thomas Ustick Walter fitted three

floors for Girard College, Philadelphia, in 1833. And then there were temple-form courthouses, markets, lunatic asylums, and – in great numbers – houses.

The temple-form house appeared in the twenties; the Lee Mansion at Arlington, Virginia, as remodeled and enlarged by George Hadfield with a tremendous portico of early Doric form in 1826, is a well-known example from that decade. Its heyday was the thirties and forties in most places; in the Deep South, where many of the larger examples belong to what has been named by Henry-Russell Hitchcock "the

6

peripteral mode" – that is, with surrounding columns but without pediments – it reigned practically unchallenged until the Civil War. At the very height of the fashion there were those who felt that the form had been devalued by excessive repetition. "One such temple well placed in a wood," remarks a character in James Fenimore Cooper's *Home as Found* (1838), "might be a pleasant object enough; but to see a river lined with them, with children trundling hoops before their doors, beef carried into their kitchens, and smoke issuing, moreover, from those unclassical objects, is too much even for a high taste."

Six of the leading architects of the Greek Revival have already been mentioned. Others of more than local importance were Robert Mills, architect of the Treasury in Washington (1836-1842) and of many other federal buildings, John Haviland, who practiced in Philadelphia and whose book *The Builder's Assistant* was the very first published in America to illustrate the Greek orders, and Isaiah Rogers of Boston, who might be called the inventor of the modern hotel. Farther west there was Gideon Shryock of Lexington, Kentucky, who built one of the few temple-form state capitols, at Frankfort, in 1826-1827; and there was Henry Walter of Cincinnati, who was responsible in some degree – though in a lesser one, it would seem, than the painter Thomas Cole – for the design of what is perhaps the finest of all the state capitols, that of Ohio at Columbus, built in 1839-1861. But the names are legion, for it was a nationwide movement. In California in 1853 there went up the last of the temple-form capitols, the Old Capitol at Benicia, a modest building with a porch having Doric columns *in antis*. In the San Francisco Mint of 1869-1874, of which A. B. Mullett was the architect, California still at the time of writing has a building that, despite the Roman Doric of its portico columns, may not improperly be described as one of the last major monuments of the Greek Revival.

Bibliography references: 1, 2, 4, 6, 7, 8, 10, 12, 20, 27, 29, 42, 50, 54, 56, 58, 59, 60, 61, 64, 65, 66, 67, 73, 75, 89

1. Belle Helene, Geismar, Louisiana. Attributed to James Gallier, Jr., circa 1845. (Library of Congress. Photo: Frances Benjamin Johnston)
2. Montgomery County Courthouse, Dayton, Ohio. Howard Daniels, architect, 1848-1850. (Photo: Hedrich-Blessing)

3. Lyle-Hunnicutt House, Athens, Georgia. Circa 1850. (Library of Congress. Photo: Frances Benjamin Johnston)
4. Church, Nepaug, Connecticut. Circa 1840. (Photo: Author)
5. Johnson House, Norwich, Connecticut. Circa 1840. (HABS, Library of Congress. Photo: Cervin Robinson)
6. House at Marlborough, Massachusetts. Circa 1845. (Photo: Author)

The Egyptian Revival

Few styles, if any, are easier to identify. Every Egyptian Revival building has one or more of the following features, and no two of them are combined in any other style: (1) battered walls; (2) the gorge and roll cornice; (3) window enframements that narrow upward; (4) columns with a more or less pronounced bulge; (5) columns that resemble bundles of stalks tied together with horizontal bands below the capitals; (6) the vulture-and-sun-disk symbol.

History: Within the Neo-Classical movement the occasional use of Egyptian forms and motifs instead of Roman or Greek – and the Egyptian Revival never amounted to much more than that – began around 1760 with Piranesi's decorations in the English Coffee House in Rome. In 1802, the publication of the work of Baron de Denon, Napoleon's archaeologist in Egypt, led to a new growth of interest in Egyptian art and architecture. However, this had a greater impact upon furniture design (in the Empire style) than upon architecture. Even in England, where the circumstance of Egyptian architecture being at once novel and very old should have recommended it to the Romantic temperament, the first Egyptian Revival building that was more than a landscape accessory did not go up until 1812. This was the Egyptian Hall on Piccadilly, London, "a permanent side-show where 32 stuffed monkeys and 11 stuffed sea lions could be seen side by side with 'an exquisite model in rice paste of the death of Voltaire by Monsieur Oudon,' a Holy Family done in wool, Mexican curiosities and an Egyptian mummy." The architect was P. F. Robinson.

In America, interest in Egyptian architecture reached a high level around 1830; in 1829, *The American Quarterly Review* devoted no less than forty pages of one issue to it. What were apparently the first three Egyptian Revival buildings here were begun in the middle thirties – all three between 1834 and 1838 – for purposes very different from those of the Egyptian Hall; they were the debtors' wing of the Philadelphia County Prison, Moyamensing, the New York Halls of Justice (better known as "the Tombs"), and the County Courthouse at Newark, New Jersey. The architect of the Philadelphia prison was Thomas U. Walter; John Haviland designed the other two buildings. They presumably chose the Egyptian style less for its exoticism, which had recommended it to

P. F. Robinson, than for its massiveness, for the New York and Newark buildings were both prisons as well as courthouses.

In the Medical College of Virginia at Richmond (Thomas S. Stewart, 1838) the style was doubtless suggested by the medical skill of the ancient Egyptians rather than by the preoccupation with corpses that the early nineteenth-century medical profession shared with them; its adoption for the entrance to the Grove Street Cemetery at New Haven, Connecticut (Henry Austin, 1845), was clearly appropriate in view of the funeral purpose of nearly all surviving Egyptian architecture. When it came to churches – such as the Whalers' Church at Sag Harbor, New York (Minard Lafever, 1845), and the First Presbyterian Church at Nashville, Tennessee (William Strickland, 1848) – Egyptian architecture was at least no less Christian than Greek was. The opportunity to display

1

50   The Egyptian Revival

the vulture and sun disk, symbol of protection, was presumably what led to the choice of Egyptian for the Pennsylvania Fire Insurance Company building on Walnut Street, Philadelphia (circa 1839). It is harder to find a good reason for its choice for the railroad station at New Bedford, Massachusetts, of which Russell Warren was the architect.

In the 1920's there was a second Egyptian Revival whose architects took advantage of the decorative potential of concrete. It flourished in the West, and Grauman's Egyptian Theater in Hollywood (Meyer and Hollar, 1922) is its most astonishing monument.

2

Bibliography references: 2, 8, 73, 94, 112

1. Moyamensing Prison, Philadelphia, Pennsylvania: Debtors' Wing. Thomas Ustick Walter, architect, 1835; demolished 1968. (HABS, Library of Congress. Photo: Jack E. Boucher)
2. Medical College of Virginia, Richmond, Virginia. Thomas S. Stewart, architect, 1838-1845. (Photo: Author)
3. House at Townsend Harbor, Massachusetts. Circa 1845. (Photo: Author)

The Early Gothic Revival

The practically universal feature of Gothic architecture is the pointed arch; other characteristic ones are pinnacles, battlements, and window tracery. In Early Gothic Revival architecture there may be no more than one or two of these features to indicate the architect's medievalizing intentions. Tracery may be of wood and of the simplest pattern, formed by twin arches within the arch of the window. Of the more complex types of tracery the commonest is that in which the mullions increase in number in the upper part of the window (that is, tracery of the English Perpendicular style), though geometrical or curvilinear patterns (Decorated) are not uncommon. Some buildings have lancet windows without tracery (Early English). (In the Early Gothic Revival the medieval prototypes are nearly always English.) For churches, the commonest plan is the basilican, with a steeple at the entrance end, though cruciform churches with a central steeple were also built. Buildings other than churches may be symmetrical or asymmetrical in plan and massing. Steep pointed gables, often with gingerbread bargeboards, are the rule; the grander houses often have a tower, or at least a turret, of square or octagonal plan. Practically every detached house has its veranda.

Many Early Gothic Revival buildings are of wood ("Carpenters' Gothic"); when of brick, they are often stuccoed. Whatever the material, the general effect is monochrome – which helps to distinguish them from buildings of High Victorian Gothic. Distinctive too is the thinness of tracery and moldings, which often results in a certain appearance of fragility.

History: By the time the Gothic Revival reached America from England, its first phase, called Gothic Rococo, was long past. And before it was in any real sense established here, Picturesque Gothic, as its second phase has been called, had achieved many of its most spectacular successes – the most spectacular of all being the prodigious Fonthill "Abbey" on the Wiltshire downs, built for William Beckford, author of *Vathek,* to the designs of James Wyatt. Nevertheless, in St. John's Cathedral at Providence, Rhode Island (John Holden Greene, 1810), America possesses one of the few known examples of the use of a Gothic "order" in the manner of Batty Langley, who had offered a full set of Gothic orders in a famous book published sixty years before. In many

54 The Early Gothic Revival

2

other buildings of the early days of the revival in America, architects clearly chose Gothic for its nonclassical forms and decoration rather than for the opportunities it offered for the "irregularity" (asymmetry) recommended by the theorists of the Picturesque movement. Examples were Sedgeley, near Philadelphia (designed by Benjamin Henry Latrobe

3

in 1799 and the first house with Gothic detail in the United States, but entirely classical in the symmetry of its elevations and its massing), the same architect's Philadelphia Bank of 1807, and William Strickland's Masonic Hall in Philadelphia of 1809. To these and other buildings of the first decade of the century may be added a much larger and more famous one of the third, namely the Eastern State Penitentiary in Philadelphia, designed by John Haviland in 1821. Despite the fact that *The Builder's Assistant* by Haviland was the first American handbook to discuss the principles of the Picturesque (as well as to contain plates of the Greek orders), this is still a classical design in Gothic disguise.

As early as 1814, a Gothic design for Columbia University was submitted by one of the professors there, James Renwick (whose architect son of the same name was to be very prominent in the revival around the middle of the century). The first educational institution actually to build in Gothic seems to have been Kenyon College, at Gambier, Ohio, in 1827-1829. Ten years later the old building of New York University went up on Washington Square, Alexander Jackson Davis being the architect. Between 1832, when he designed Glen Ellen near Baltimore for a client fresh from a visit to Sir Walter Scott at Abbotsford, and the Civil War, when he retired from practice, Davis was the most prolific architect of Gothic country houses in America. Major works by him that have survived to the present are Lyndhurst, at Tarrytown, New York (1838, with later additions also by Davis), and Belmead, in Powhatan County, Virginia (1845). He was also the originator of a much smaller type of country house, or cottage, characterized by steep roofs, a dominant central gable, and spacious verandas. This was popularized by his friend the landscape gardener and horticulturalist Andrew Jackson Downing in his *Cottage Residences,* to which Davis contributed designs. Of Downing it has been said that he naturalized the Picturesque in the United States; his books were immensely influential in forming mid-nineteenth-century taste. *Cottage Residences,* first published in 1842, was reissued no less than twelve times down to 1888, with the result that versions of Davis's cottage "in the English or Rural Gothic Style" (as Downing described it) were built from Maine to California.

For Davis, as for most of his contemporaries in America, "picturesque effect" was all. His larger country houses might be free from the gingerbread bargeboards of his cottages, but they showed less knowledge of medieval architecture than Wyatt's houses had in England forty and fifty years before. Nor do the Gothic houses of Richard Upjohn show much more. Some of Upjohn's churches, on the other hand, are among the very few American buildings that could have been taken seriously by the English critics of the 1840's when new standards of archaeological

4

5

accuracy and liturgical correctness were being promulgated – most effectively by the Anglican Cambridge Camden Society, through its magazine *The Ecclesiologist,* and by the Catholic convert Augustus Welby Northmore Pugin, through both his books and his buildings. Upjohn's best-known church is Trinity, New York (1839-1846); his most attractive is perhaps St. Mary's, Burlington, New Jersey (1846-1848). Trinity is in the latest of the English Gothic styles, Perpendicular, while the Burlington church is in the earliest, Early English. The medieval style that was admired most by the English ecclesiologists – by some of them to the exclusion of all others – was the Decorated, which came between. This was the style chosen by James Renwick, Jr., for Grace Church, New York (1843-1846), and by John Notman for St. Mark's, Philadelphia (1847-1849), to name two other well-known churches of this phase of the Gothic Revival. The parish buildings adjoining the Philadelphia church, which are also the work of Notman, are a good example of the application to secular design of Pugin's principles, which were functional

6

and anti-Picturesque – for Pugin insisted that the picturesque qualities of medieval buildings were by-products of their essential functionalism and thus not to be imitated for their own sake.

Bibliography references: 1, 2, 4, 10, 42, 46, 61, 71, 88

1. Christ Church, Binghamton, New York. Richard Upjohn, architect, 1853-1855. (HABS, Library of Congress. Photo: Jack E. Boucher)
2. Loudoun, Lexington, Kentucky. John McMurtry, architect, circa 1850. (HABS, Library of Congress. Photo: Lester Jones)
3. Congregational Church, Ipswich, Massachusetts. 1847; destroyed by fire 1965. (Photo: Author)
4. St. James, Wilmington, North Carolina. Thomas U. Walter, architect, 1839. (Library of Congress. Photo: Frances Benjamin Johnston)
5. St. Mary's, Burlington, New Jersey. Richard Upjohn, architect, 1846-1848. (HABS, Library of Congress. Photo: Nathaniel R. Ewan)
6. Rotch House, New Bedford, Massachusetts. Alexander Jackson Davis, architect, 1846. (HABS, Library of Congress. Photo: Ned Goode)

The Romanesque Revival

This was the revival of the round-arched medieval style that preceded the pointed-arched Gothic. Semicircular arches are used for all openings and sometimes where there are no openings, in series as a form of wall enrichment; in such cases the arches may intersect one another. Nearly always the round-arch form is repeated in miniature in the arcaded corbel table. Under stringcourses and eaves, including the raking eaves of the gables, this is a feature – and may on occasion be the only feature – which distinguishes the Romanesque from other round-arched styles (such as Italian Villa). Buttresses are normally of slighter projection than in Gothic. Towers may be finished off with parapets or topped with pyramidal roofs or – though these are strictly speaking Gothic – with spires. A favorite form of tower roof is pyramidal with concave slopes. Massing may be symmetrical or asymmetrical; in churches with two-towered façades one tower is often taller than the other. The wheel window (really a Gothic feature, like the spire, but with precedents in the late Romanesque architecture of Italy) is common. Wall surfaces are broad and smooth.

History: The Romanesque Revival began in the mid-1840's, and its success was such that in the 1850's and 1860's new churches and public buildings – but not houses – were more frequently Romanesque than Gothic. On the face of it this is rather surprising because in England, which the United States still generally followed in matters of architectural taste, the case was quite otherwise, with the Romanesque Revival forming a minor and indeed almost negligible incident. In France, however, Gothic designs were far outnumbered by Romanesque ones during the same decades, while in Germany, whose stock was high in mid-nineteenth-century America, a revival of the Romanesque that had started in Munich around 1830, as the earliest in Europe, was far from being spent. It should be remembered, also, that the odor of sanctity that recommended Gothic to Pugin and the English ecclesiologists was less perceptible on this side of the Atlantic. In the eyes of most Americans, Gothic was still primarily a mode of the Picturesque – and it soon became apparent that Romanesque lent itself equally well to Picturesque effects. Nor is it unlikely that many American architects were happy to find that Romanesque was free from that peculiar difficulty of Gothic

which had led the English architect John Nash to exclaim, "I hate this Gothic style; one window costs more trouble than two houses ought to."

However, the first two architects to design Romanesque buildings in America, Richard Upjohn and James Renwick, were more skilled in Gothic tracery than most of their contemporaries. Upjohn's Romanesque Church of the Pilgrims in Brooklyn, New York, went up in 1844-1846, and 1846 was the year in which Renwick designed the Church of the Pilgrims in New York City and the first great secular monument of the revival, the Smithsonian Institution in Washington. The latter was a building that showed how Picturesque the Romanesque could be – and in the national stronghold of classicism too! That the Norman style, as it was called in this case, had many other virtues was soon explained, with Renwick's assistance, by Robert Dale Owen in *Hints on Public Architecture, Containing, among Illustrations, Views and Plans of the Smithsonian Institution,* published in 1849. Owen does not disdain to use, in an indirect way, what one may call the Nash argument against Gothic, stating that the Norman style "has fewer members and less complication of details." It was also – and this surely was an important consideration in the establishment of the style – more democratic. "Its entire expression is less ostentatious, and if political character may be ascribed to Architecture, more republican."

The Romanesque went under several other names during the years of the revival. "Round Style" was a safe, all-inclusive one favored by the Congregational Churches. However, use of the term "Norman" did not necessarily narrow the field of precedent down even to that worked by Renwick for the Smithsonian; still less did it imply the use of detail as "archaeologizing" as that of John Notman's Church of the Holy Trinity in Philadelphia. One of the few "Norman villas" actually built – many house pattern books included the genre – was Bartram Hall, near Philadelphia, built to the design of Samuel Sloan in 1851, and this was nothing but an Italian Villa made "Norman" with arcaded corbel tables in place of bracketed cornices and a high concave-sided roof on the tower.

Another name for the Romanesque was "Lombard." This is accurate enough when applied, for example, to Thomas A. Tefft's Union Station of 1848 at Providence, Rhode Island (which is to be regarded as one of the triumphs of the revival if one agrees with Hitchcock that it was

64 The Romanesque Revival

2

"without much question the finest early station in the New World"). However, it was applied to things of quite other kinds as well. As a rule, the architects of the Romanesque Revival were more interested in novelty than in scholarship. Norman features might appear in "Lombard" designs, and Lombard in "Norman," while the prevailing character of many designs (notably those of Leopold Eidlitz) was actually German. What did not appear until the 1870's, when the Romanesque Revival reached a new phase to be discussed under a separate head, was the influence of Spain and the South of France.

Bibliography references: 10, 109

1. Holy Trinity, Philadelphia, Pennsylvania. John Notman, architect, 1857. (Photo: Author)
2. Old Stone Church, Cleveland, Ohio. Charles Heard, architect, circa 1855. (HABS, Library of Congress. Photo: Martin Lindsey)
3. St. Patrick's Church, Chicago, Illinois. 1854; belfries later. (HABS, Library of Congress. Photo: Cervin Robinson)
4. Church of the Assumption, St. Paul, Minnesota. Joseph Reidl, architect, 1870-1874. (HABS, Library of Congress. Photo: Jack E. Boucher)

The Italian Villa Style

A tower of square or (more rarely) octagonal plan is a feature of most buildings in this style; usually it stands off-center, often at a corner. Failing a tower, there is likely to be a cupola or glazed belvedere. Buildings consist of well-defined rectilinear blocks, as a rule asymmetrically grouped although the elevations of the individual blocks are symmetrical. Wall surfaces are smooth and uniform, with rustication, when present, confined to the quoins. Roofs are of slight pitch, gabled or hipped or both; the eaves, which may be of considerable projection, are usually supported by brackets. Windows typically are round-headed and are often grouped in twos or threes; in the earlier examples of the style they are simple apertures without any sort of enframement, or framed with a flat architrave at most; later, more elaborate treatments, with hoodmolds or even pediments, came into use. Bay windows are common features, as also are balustraded balconies, and houses nearly always have a veranda or loggia.

History: The Italian Villa Style was originally inspired by the anonymous or "vernacular" farmhouse architecture of the Italian countryside. This had gone unnoticed by architects and men of taste until the end of the eighteenth century, when its asymmetry or "irregularity" – a quality due in most cases to the buildings in question having been added to from time to time through the centuries – caught the attention of the devotees of the Picturesque. In 1802, John Nash, who was to be George IV's favorite architect, designed the first English house in the style, namely Cronkhill, near Shrewsbury. Before the end of the second decade of the century Italian villas were appearing in the company of the Gothic and Grecian residences in the design books, and by the 1830's the Italian Villa Style had become the preponderant non-Gothic style of the Picturesque movement.

In the United States its day dawned in 1837, when the Scottish-born architect John Notman built an Italian villa for Bishop Doane at Burlington, New Jersey. Four years later this house was published and described by Andrew Jackson Downing in his *Treatise on the Theory and Practice of Landscape Gardening, Adapted to North America,* and Downing went on to help popularize the style by publishing designs for Italian villas by Alexander Jackson Davis in both *Cottage Residences* (1842) and *The Architecture of Country Houses* (1850). The Italian Villa Style was recommended by Downing as being at once picturesque and practical. On the one hand, "the irregularity in the masses of the edifice and the shape of the roof" rendered "the sky outline of a building in this style extremely picturesque"; on the other, the style allowed exceptional freedom in planning:

"A villa, however small, in the Italian style, may have an elegant and expressive character, without interfering with convenient internal arrangement, while at the same time, this style has the very great merit of allowing additions to be made in almost any direction, without injuring the effect of the original structure; indeed such is the variety of sizes and forms, which the different parts of the Italian villa may take, in perfect accordance with architectural propriety, that the original edifice frequently gains in beauty by additions of this description."

This, after all, though Downing does not say so, was how its Italian prototype had gained in its particular kind of picturesque beauty.

Curiously often, an Italian Villa design would be directly reproduced in a later building but reversed left to right. Henry Austin, in the Norton House at New Haven, Connecticut, built a looking-glass version of a design published by Downing; Richard Upjohn reversed the design of the Edward King House at Newport, Rhode Island, which he did in 1845, for Homewood Villa in Baltimore six years later. Calvert Vaux in his *Villas and Cottages* illustrates two houses built simultaneously in Georgetown, in which reversal of plan was resorted to because the two clients "desired to obtain the particular distribution of the rooms shown on the plan . . . although the situations on which the buildings were to be erected differed somewhat in their local requirements."

Occasionally the Italian Villa Style was employed for buildings other than houses, good examples being the City Hall at Utica, New York (Upjohn, 1852), and Calvert Street Station, Baltimore (C. R. Niernsee, circa 1855, destroyed 1950).

Bibliography references: 1, 2, 10, 56, 88, 108

1. Camden, Caroline County, Virginia. Nathan G. Starkweather, architect, 1857. (HABS, Library of Congress. Photo: Thomas T. Waterman)
2. Jarrard House, New Brunswick, New Jersey. 1866-1874. (HABS, Library of Congress. Photo: Jack E. Boucher)
3. Morse-Libby House, Portland, Maine. Henry Austin, architect, 1859. (HABS, Library of Congress)
4. Calvert Station, Baltimore, Maryland. John R. Niernsée, architect, 1855; demolished 1950. (HABS, Library of Congress. Photo: E. H. Pickering)

1

The Renaissance Revival: The Romano-Tuscan Mode

Straight-fronted buildings – cubic blocks when freestanding – without any considerable projections or recessions in the main mass are the rule. Columns, if present, are confined to porches or window tabernacle frames. A massive cornice (*cornicione* in the prototypes), sometimes scaled to the full height of the building, is the crowning feature; the roof behind it is low and invisible to the spectator in the street. Elevations are symmetrical. Apart from rusticated quoins, and sometimes a rusticated ground story, the wall surfaces are usually smooth and plain, serving as a neutral background for windows, doorways, and (in many cases) balustraded balconies. The windows, which are often linked horizontally by stringcourses, are normally trabeated. They may vary in height from story to story, those of the second story, which in the Italian city palace contained the rooms of state, being the tallest. The second-story windows may also be more elaborately treated – perhaps with a complete entablature above each – while the other windows are framed in architraves alone. In houses, clubs, and public buildings the windows tend to be widely spaced; in commercial buildings the window area may be much increased.

History: The revival of the astylar Italian palace of High Renaissance Rome and Florence was initiated in 1829 by Charles Barry, later to be the architect of the Houses of Parliament. The building with which he did so was the Travellers' Club on Pall Mall, London, a free adaptation of the Pandolfini Palace by Raphael in Florence. Before the thirties were over, Barry had designed two more High Renaissance clubhouses, the Manchester Athenaeum and the larger and better-known Reform Club, which stands, a smaller and neater Farnese Palace, next door to the Travellers'.

One of the first two major American buildings in the style was also a clubhouse, the Philadelphia Athenaeum; its architect was John Notman, who had designed the first house in the Italian Villa style in the United States, and it went up in 1845-1847. The other, begun in the same year, was a dry goods store, the long-destroyed A. T. Stewart Downtown Store in New York; this very large five-story commercial palace, which created a sensation in its day, is attributed to an Italian marble cutter, Ottavian Gori.

76 The Renaissance Revival: The Romano-Tuscan Mode

Unlike Italian Villa, the astylar Renaissance mode was nonpicturesque, one might say antipicturesque, and in intention, academic. So it is not surprising that in a country to which the delights of the Picturesque had been revealed so recently, and one whose architects were not often academically inclined, examples as "correct" as the Philadelphia Athenaeum should have remained rather few and far between. However, the general idea was not hard to get and was the more acceptable in that it promised dignity without the expense of columns. By elaborating the window frames and crowding the windows, it could be given a certain richness, although it could never compete with the North Italian mode in this respect. The style had its run in federal buildings under Ammi B. Young in the 1850's – for example, the Georgetown, D.C., Custom House (now Post Office). At the other

2

3

end of the scale miles of mid-century row houses, including New York brownstones by the hundred, owe their character to its impact upon the Georgian tradition in row-house design.

Bibliography references: 10, 56, 73, 117, 120

1. Athenaeum of Philadelphia, Philadelphia, Pennsylvania. John Notman, architect, 1845-1847. (Atwater Kent Museum)
2. India House, Hanover Square, New York. Circa 1850. (Nicholson and Galloway)
3. Custom House (now Post Office), Georgetown, D.C. Ammi B. Young, architect, 1857. (HABS, Library of Congress. Photo: John D. Brostrup)

1

The Renaissance Revival: The North Italian Mode

In general form, buildings of this Renaissance Revival mode resemble those of the Romano-Tuscan, and like them they have symmetrical elevations crowned with bold cornices. But windows are always arched, and they tend to be, or at least to seem, larger; there is a minimum of unbroken wall surface. The over-all effect is decidedly richer, with strong contrasts of light and shade. This may be due to sculptural ornament, to the use of superimposed orders (one to each story), to paneling and layering of the wall surfaces, or to a combination of these factors.

History: The North Italian Renaissance Revival appeared in the United States in 1850, some five years later than the Romano-Tuscan, when R. G. Hatfield designed the Sun Building, Baltimore. This was in the distinctive style of Sansovino, best known as the architect of St. Mark's Library in Venice (1536), in which the motif of the Roman Colosseum – arched openings framed between columns with a full entablature to each story – is employed in an extremely ornate and full-bodied form. The Sansovinesque had made its first appearance in England in 1847, when Sydney Smirke designed a new front for the Carlton Club, immediately to the west of Barry's Reform Club. It was a style in which an architect could cater to the growing taste for richness and relief that was already beginning to make the Romano-Tuscan mode seem rather plain. In the Sun Building Hatfield was able to employ a material, too, that catered to that taste by facilitating the mass production of elaborate ornament – cast iron – and not only for the ornament, for this was one of the first buildings with façades entirely of cast iron to come out of the New York factory of James Bogardus. Cast iron also facilitated the enlargement of the windows, so desirable in a newspaper building, and Hatfield's manner of doing this within the Sansovinesque formula was successful enough to be repeated in 1854 in the Harper Brothers Building in New York, in its day perhaps the most famous of all Bogardus's iron buildings. A fine though somewhat less elaborate example of the iron-fronted Sansovinesque, the Haughwout Building of 1857, manufactured to the design of the architect J. P. Gaynor by Bogardus's rival Daniel Badger, still stands on the corner of Broadway and Broome Street in New York.

2

3

On the West Coast the Sansovinesque was most grandly represented, from 1866 until the fire of 1906, by the Bank of California in San Francisco, designed by David Farquharson, a Scottish architect who had arrived in the Gold Rush of '49. This was a solid masonry building; and solid is the word, for each of its forty-two columns was a monolith weighing between three and four tons.

The North Italian Renaissance mode was far from being all Sansovinesque. Fifteenth-century Venice contributed, on occasion, its classicized window tracery; sometimes there are features that could have come from Sansovino's Veronese contemporary, Sanmicheli. In many cases the biggest contribution was that of the nineteenth century itself – notably in those cast-iron fronts of extreme openness in which the arches, semicircular or segmental, spring from slender columns that make little pretense of belonging to any of the recognized classical orders.

Bibliography references: 10, 56, 61, 63, 73, 117

1. Haughwout Building, New York City. J. P. Gaynor, architect, 1857. (Photo: Cervin Robinson)
2. Farmers' and Mechanics' Bank (now Philadelphia Maritime Museum), Philadelphia, Pennsylvania. John M. Gries, architect, 1855. (Photo: Author)
3. George Gordon Building, Philadelphia, Pennsylvania. 1856; demolished 1963. (HABS, Library of Congress. Photo: Cervin Robinson)

The Octagon Mode

The Octagon Mode house is built to the plan of a regular octagon and is from two to four stories high. The roof is flat or low and is often surmounted by a belvedere. There may be a porch to the front door only, or the building may be surrounded by verandas with galleries above. Detail may be of the utmost plainness, or of a Greek Revival, Italian Villa, or Gothic Revival character.

1

History: All but a handful of the octagonal houses in the United States were built between 1848 and 1860 and were inspired by a book entitled *A Home for All or the Gravel Wall and Octagon Mode of Building,* which reached a sixth edition eight years after its first publication in 1848. The author was Orson Squire Fowler, a phrenologist and a prolific writer on health and happiness – marital happiness in particular. Titles of some of his other books are *Love and Parentage Applied to the Improvement of Offspring; Marriage, Its History and Philosophy; Matrimony, or Phrenology and Physiology Applied to the Selection of Congenial Companions for Life;* and *Sexual Science.* He himself married three times.

3

The prime advantage of the octagonal plan, according to Fowler, is that it encloses one fifth more floor area than a square with the same total length of wall. "Scarcely less important" is its greater beauty, which is due to its approaching more closely to the sphere, "the predominant or governing form of Nature." Then it makes for better heating and more compact internal planning. "What a vast number of steps will the octagon save a large and stirring family over the square!" Fowler demonstrates this saving with dotted lines on his plans. (Can these be the first published circulation diagrams in history?)

Fowler's "gravel wall" was "made wholly out of lime and stones, sand included, which is of course fine stone." That is to say, it was concrete. His own house at Fishkill, of four stories surmounted by a cupola and containing sixty-five rooms, was of concrete, and he thought it the perfect building material. He was willing to allow the use on occasion of other materials and methods of construction, including board and plank walls, but like Jefferson before him he was an enemy of the frame building.

Houses in the Octagon Mode were built throughout the length and breadth of the United States. A count made twenty years ago showed New York, with twenty-five, as the state then possessing the most surviving examples; Massachusetts took second place, with twenty-one, and Wisconsin third, with nineteen.

Bibliography references: 65, 67, 93

1. Octagon House, Elkhorn, Wisconsin. Circa 1855. (HABS, Library of Congress. Photo: Roy Johnson)
2. Cedar Point, Swansboro, North Carolina. Circa 1855. (Library of Congress. Photo: Frances Benjamin Johnston)
3. Langworthy House, Dubuque, Iowa. Circa 1855. (HABS, Library of Congress. Photo: Harry N. Bevers)

3: Styles That Reached Their Zenith in 1860-1890

The epithet High Victorian may be used in a general way of all the architecture of the 1860's and 1870's as well as, more narrowly, of the Gothic and Italianate of these decades. Height in the literal sense – tall proportions – was one quality common to most buildings; others were variety of color and surface textures and a calculated restlessness. Forms from different sources in the past were often brought together in a single design, to result in what has been named "synthetic eclecticism." In the 1880's a reaction in favor of quieter and more homogeneous effects set in.

High Victorian Gothic

In High Victorian Gothic the standard features of all Gothic architecture are employed, but with effects altogether different from those of the Early Gothic Revival. The medieval models are no longer almost exclusively English, and they are hardly ever Perpendicular. Italy, France, and Germany all contribute to the stock of forms. However, the basic differences between High Victorian Gothic and the earlier style are more than differences in derivation. One of the most obvious is in the matter of color; High Victorian Gothic is polychrome, or at least bichrome. The variegation is produced by the use of combinations of structural or facing materials; two kinds of stone are used in one wall or alternate in the window arches, brickwork is banded with stone, walls of red brick are diapered with black, columns of pink or gray granite stand out against the limestone or sandstone behind them. Then the details – moldings, tracery, carved ornament – are heavier and fatter; the extreme toward which they all tend (and at which not a few arrive) is coarseness and not, as in the earlier style, fragility. Indeed, fragile is the last adjective anyone would use for these buildings; their solidity, which is often real as well as apparent, is emphasized by various means, notably the treatment of the windows, which are set well back from the plane of the wall.

External woodwork is solid and structural-seeming; when it appears in the gable end of a roof, it is as framing and not gingerbread ornament. Roof lines are more complex than in the Early Gothic Revival, often breaking out into a profusion of gablets and dormers. Spires are less slender than those of the earlier style. Towers often have an overhanging top stage. Top-heavy effects in general are common. So are strong scale contrasts, with large and small features of the same kind and similar design side by side or confronting each other.

History: In the United States, High Victorian Gothic was for the most part a post-bellum phenomenon. Its heyday came in the seventies here, whereas in England (its homeland, as its name indicates) most of its representative works date from the sixties. In England the first High Victorian Gothic building was designed in 1849; this was the church of All Saints, Margaret Street, London, by William Butterfield. In America, the first, the Nott Memorial Library at Union College, Schenectady,

was designed by Edward T. Potter in 1856; the first ecclesiastical buildings in the style did not go up until after the Civil War. One of its major monuments – and one that is more than a little ecclesiastical in appearance – is another building for an institution of higher learning, Memorial Hall of Harvard University, which was built to the design of Henry Van Brunt in 1870-1878. (Van Brunt's partner was William Robert Ware, who in 1865 founded the first school of architecture in the United States, that of the Massachusetts Institute of Technology.)

The philosopher of High Victorian Gothic, although he came to despise the movement, was John Ruskin (who during his lifetime was read even more in America than in his native England). Ruskin's first

3

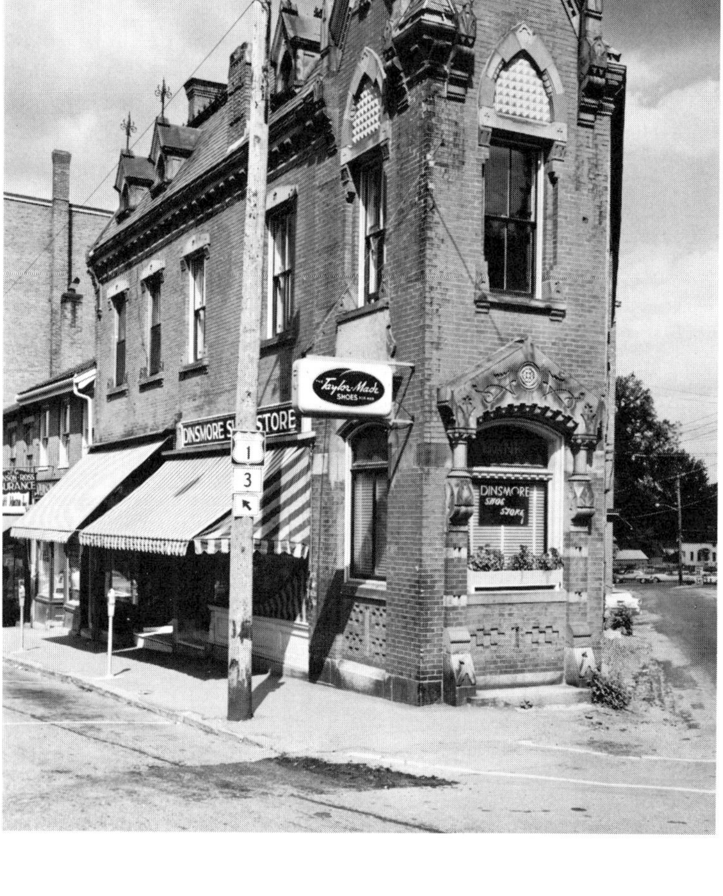
Taylor-Made
SHOES
DINSMORE SHOE STORE
DINSMORE
SHOE
STORE
1
3

4

book on architecture, *The Seven Lamps of Architecture,* was published in 1849. In it he proposed principles for the use of color in architecture that were subsequently adopted by the architects of the High Victorian Gothic and underlie many of the most characteristic effects of the style. (Whether Butterfield adopted them or arrived at them independently, while designing All Saints', Margaret Street, in the year of the publication of *The Seven Lamps,* is a moot point.) Color, for Ruskin, is good. But it must not be applied color. It must be integral with the materials used in the construction or finishing of the building; hence the variety of stones, the bands or patterns of red and black and yellow brick, the alternating colors (or even materials) of the voussoirs of the arches that help so conspicuously to distinguish High Victorian Gothic from earlier phases of the revival. "Constructional coloration" and "permanent polychrome" were the names for it all.

The Early Gothic Revival had sought inspiration in English medieval architecture almost exclusively. The High Victorians broadened their eclecticism to borrow from continental Europe. In *The Seven Lamps* Ruskin had come down on the side of English Gothic as the style to be generally used as a basis for future development; with his later book, *The Stones of Venice,* he did much to redress the balance in favor of the Continent. The National Academy in New York, built to the design of Peter B. Wight in 1862-1865, was a version, enormously admired in its day, of Ruskin's beloved Doges' Palace; a later and better example of Italian Gothic was the old Boston Museum of Fine Arts (Sturgis and Brigham, 1876-1878), which displayed an unprecedented quantity of external terra-cotta decoration (all made in England). Nevertheless, most of the detail of High Victorian Gothic turns out on examination to have English prototypes, when it has any prototypes at all. That one should have to examine it to ascertain this is a measure of the independence of the style, which was essentially unimitative and "contemporary."

Few people today would readily use the adjective "beautiful" of High Victorian Gothic architecture. But then beauty was rather suspect when that architecture was new, as it has been in more recent times; it was tainted by association with the Greek Revival, for one thing. The qualities that were most admired and sought in architecture by the High Victorians were "truth," "reality," and "character." These terms,

so much more easily understood than defined, did not take long to cross the Atlantic after achieving currency in England. As early as 1848 an English-born and English-trained architect, Frank Wills, gave a lecture at the first meeting of the New York Ecclesiological Society with the title "Reality in Architecture." By and large, "truth" and "reality" meant much the same thing; thus the American writer Horace B. Wallace, in an account of his European travels published in 1855, says that Gothic decoration "is derived out of reality, and is representative of truth." "Character" was a word with a century-old tradition of use in architectural contexts. Its meaning had changed, however. To say that a building had the requisite character no longer meant, as it had in the eighteenth century and in the earlier years of the nineteenth, that its design expressed, or its style was suitable for, its function. It meant that it possessed the attributes of a man who, as we say, has character – forcefulness, and the other qualities that make their possessor hard to overlook or to forget. No buildings anywhere ever had more character in this sense than those of Frank Furness in Philadelphia – for example, the Pennsylvania Academy of the Fine Arts (1872-1876).

Bibliography references: 4, 7, 10, 18, 62, 71, 75, 91

1. Pennsylvania Academy of Fine Arts, Philadelphia, Pennsylvania. Frank Furness, architect, 1876. (Photo: Author)
2. Camillus Baptist Church, Camillus, New York. Archimedes Russell, architect, 1879-1880. (New York State Council on the Arts. Photo: Gilbert Ask)
3. Converse House, Norwich, Connecticut. Circa 1870. (HABS, Library of Congress. Photo: Cervin Robinson)
4. Belfast National Bank, Belfast, Maine. George M. Harding, architect, 1878-1879. (HABS, Library of Congress. Photo: Cervin Robinson)
5. Syracuse Savings Bank, Syracuse, New York. Joseph L. Silsbee, architect, 1876. (New York State Council on the Arts. Photo: Gilbert Ask)
6. Jefferson Market Courthouse (Jefferson Market Branch Library), New York City. Frederick C. Withers and Calvert Vaux, architects, 1875. (HABS, Library of Congress. Photo: Cervin Robinson)

High Victorian Italianate

It is by the treatment of the windows that High Victorian Italianate may, as a rule, be told most readily from earlier and later Italianate styles. Three distinctive devices are employed: (1) the stilted segmental arch, or *straight-sided arch,* in which the arch proper springs from a point some way above the capital or other impost feature, with which it is linked by a vertical continuation of the architrave molding; (2) the *flat-topped arch,* in which the relative positions of the curves and straight lines are reversed; (3) the *rectangular arch* (so to call it), which is produced by bending an architrave molding around the upper third of a rectangular aperture. Trabeated or arched windows of conventional design may appear in association with any of these devices. When there is a full order, with columns supporting an entablature, the latter

1

is often stilted in a manner analagous to (1) by means of brackets or a thickening of the architrave over each column. The same tendency to verticalize classical features is seen in the overscaled brackets of crowning cornices, which are often thrust up into pedimental forms that are unrelated to anything in the façades below. The general effect of High Victorian Italianate façades, with their profusion of shadow-forming moldings, variform openings, and small-scale ornament (often of cast iron) is busy, not to say crowded. The character of the ornament ranges from out-and-out naturalism to a stylization of already stylized classical forms, such as the Greek anthemion.

History: Like High Victorian Gothic, with which it is approximately coeval, High Victorian Italianate is the result of the transformation of an earlier revival by architects whose ideals were anything but revivalist. "Character," which meant the same thing for them as it did for their colleagues of the Gothic persuasion, was the chief of those ideals. "Truth," to judge from the readiness with which they employed cast-iron ornament, anathema to the Goths, was much less their concern. Nor did constructional coloration have any important place in their philosophy of design.

But then they were not a philosophical group. They were practical men, for High Victorian Italianate was the practical style of the day. It was not an ecclesiastical or a governmental style but a domestic and (above all) commercial one. It is tempting to call it the commercial vernacular of the High Victorian decades – until one remembers Sir John Summerson's observation that the use of the word "vernacular" by historians is a confession of ignorance. And certainly our ignorance of the matters that, were we not ignorant of them, would make us less ready to use the word in connection with High Victorian Italianate, is profound. We can rarely name the architects who worked in it – let alone assess their relative importance. As for the sources of the style, and the means by which it drew from them, here is a case of "synthetic eclecticism" that would surely repay some investigation, although a full analysis might indeed prove tedious. The most that one can safely say, as things are, is that the generally Italianate nature of this architecture is often tempered by an infusion of French influence – from that of Louis XIV Baroque to that of the then recent Néo-Grec.

One of the characteristic features of the style – and one that was clearly thought especially conducive to "character" too – has indeed been given some attention, by the writer just named. This is the stilted segmental arch, or straight-sided arch (as we have chosen to call it). Summerson has traced this back to 1840, in England, when a form of it was employed by the learned and respectable classicist, Charles Robert Cockerell, in an insurance building in the City of London. By 1853, he tells us, it "had begun to spread like a drug habit," the reason for its popularity being that "it distorted convention, crashed through the rules of taste, was 'self made'; it gave an expression of structural frankness, assigning to the ornamental attributes of architecture a sub-

3

sidiary, merely pretty, role." It was, in short, thoroughly democratic (in the special American sense) and thus assured of the hearty reception this country gave to it when it crossed the Atlantic.

Bibliography references: High Victorian Italianate still awaits its literature. The quotation in the text is taken from J. Summerson, "The London Suburban Villa," *Architectural Review* (London), CIV (August 1948), 63-72 (not listed in the bibliography because its subject matter is not American).

1. Blagen Block, Portland, Oregon. Completed 1888. (Photo: Edmund Y. Lee)
2. Store, Main Street, Poughkeepsie, New York. 1872. (Photo: Author)
3. Marks House, Portland, Oregon. Attributed to Warren Haywood Williams, architect, 1882. (Oregon Historical Society. Photo: William Bryan)

The Second Empire Style

The hallmark of the style is the high mansard roof, with a curb around the top of the visible slopes. Dormer windows are universal, both wall dormers and roof dormers being employed (sometimes in the same building); they take many shapes, including the circular. The chimneys are important elements in the composition of the upper part of the building and are classically detailed. In larger buildings projecting pavilions, central or terminal or both, are usual; each pavilion has its own roof, sometimes with convex slopes. Superimposed orders occur sometimes; the colossal order was not employed. In general, buildings of the Second Empire style are tall, boldly modeled, and emphatically three-dimensional in effect.

History: The style takes its name from the French Second Empire, the reign of Napoleon III (1852-1870). One of the first great public works of the Second Empire in Paris was the vast extension to the Palace of the Louvre built in 1852-1857. Known as the New Louvre, this is in a heavier, more sculptural version of the style of the seventeenth-century parts of the palace; the architects were L.-T.-J. Visconti and H.-M. Lefuel.

The New Louvre was the central building of the Second Empire style. However, its influence in America was more often than not indirect. Designs inspired by it that were entered in the competition for a new foreign office and a new war office in London in 1857 were illustrated more widely, and therefore imitated more frequently, than the Parisian prototype. Neither this nor the fact that a handful of designs possessing the characteristics of the style had been executed (in France, England, and the United States) before Napoleon was proclaimed Emperor detracts from the propriety of the designation Second Empire Style. Certainly any alternative referring to its seventeenth-century sources would be less suitable, for in Hitchcock's words, "it was a consciously 'modern' movement, deriving its prestige from contemporary Paris, not from any period of the past like the Greek, the Gothic, or even the Renaissance Revivals." As for an alternative in current if limited use, "General Grant," although it indicates accurately enough the heyday of the style for public buildings (Grant's presidency, 1869-1877), it fails to acknowledge the international background of the style.

James Renwick, the pioneer of the Romanesque Revival, was the architect of two of the first major nondomestic buildings of the Second Empire Style – the Corcoran Gallery (now Court of Claims), Washington, in 1859, and the Main Hall of Vassar College, near Poughkeepsie, New York, in 1860. The model for the latter was not the New Louvre but, on the client's insistence, the sixteenth-century Palace of the Tuileries, which as Napoleon III's official residence was almost as much a symbol of contemporary Paris. In 1862 the first commercial building in the style, the Continental Life Insurance Company Building in New York, was designed by Griffith Thomas, and work began on the building whose example made it the favorite style for public buildings, namely Boston City Hall, by Gridley Bryant and Arthur Gilman, who claimed that the style was one that grew "naturally out of the character and requirements of the structure." Gilman subsequently became consultant to the office of the architect responsible for most of the big

The Second Empire Style

federal buildings during the Grant administration, Alfred B. Mullett, and he is thought to have been the actual designer of many of them – including the Executive Office Building (originally the State, War, and Navy Building) of 1871-1875. Another surviving Second Empire work from Mullett's office, and a powerful one, is the Old Post Office (originally the Federal Building and Customs House) at St. Louis,

Missouri. Philadelphia City Hall, whose architect was John McArthur, Jr., grandfather of the general, is the largest American building in the style and was for a period the largest building in the United States; the cornerstone was laid in 1874, and the statue of William Penn was placed on top of the tower just twenty years later, though the building was in use by 1881.

Few American cities are without houses in the Second Empire style, which got a hold in domestic architecture in the middle fifties. Most are "Americanized" by spacious porches or verandas, and many, in consequence of their architects having deferred to practical requirements or a taste for the picturesque (or both), are asymmetric in their massing.

Bibliography references: 7, 10, 50, 52, 56, 62

1. City Hall, Philadelphia, Pennsylvania. John McArthur, Jr., architect, 1871-1881. (Photo: Author)
2. City Hall, Boston, Massachusetts. Bryant and Gilman, architects, 1862-1865. (HABS, Library of Congress. Photo: Cervin Robinson)
3. Smith House, New Brunswick, New Jersey. Circa 1875. (HABS, Library of Congress. Photo: Jack E. Boucher)
4. Bain House, St. Louis, Missouri. George I. Barnett, architect, 1870. (HABS, Library of Congress. Photo: Paul Piaget)
5. Gallatin House (latterly Governor's Mansion), Sacramento, California. Nathaniel Goodell, architect, 1877-1878. (HABS, Library of Congress. Photo: Jack E. Boucher)

The Stick Style

Stick Style buildings have tall proportions with high, steep roofs, frequently of complex plan and irregular silhouette; the eaves are of considerable projection and are supported by large brackets; often there is exposed framing in the gable end of a roof. Verandas are extensive, their roofs being carried on posts with diagonal braces. Diagonal "stickwork" is one of the most characteristic features of the style. Walls may be faced with vertical boards and battens or (in the final development of the style) with horizontal clapboards having an overlay of other boards – vertical and horizontal, and sometimes diagonal too – that suggest or symbolize the unseen structural frame.

History: Although in its earlier manifestations it often owed something to the Swiss chalet and although Gothic forms, or at least allusions, appeared in it throughout its life, the Stick Style may be counted with the Shingle Style as one of the two most purely American styles of the nineteenth century. As Vincent Scully (who named it) has shown, premonitions of the style are found in designs published by Andrew Jackson Downing in 1850. Basic to the development of its theory was Downing's insistence upon "truthfulness" in wooden construction, which in his view was to be achieved, for example, by the use of vertical boarding on the outside of walls (because "the main timbers which enter into the frame of a wooden house and support the structure are vertical, and hence the vertical boarding properly signifies to the eye a wooden house"). It was in the quarter-century between Downing's death in 1851 and the Philadelphia Centennial Exposition of 1876 that the Stick Style flourished. At the Centennial itself several states, including New Jersey, Illinois, and Michigan, were represented by well-developed examples of it.

Besides exhibiting "truthfulness," the Stick Style was admirably well adapted, in the opinion of its users, to the cultivation of "character" (for which, see the section on High Victorian Gothic). "The strength and character of a building depend almost wholly on the shadows which are thrown upon its surface by projecting members," declared Henry W. Cleaveland in *Village and Farm Cottages* (1856), one of the most successful of the pattern books containing Stick Style designs. And Stick Style architects discovered that there was hardly a member that could not, in a pinch, be made to project.

An important pioneer of the Stick Style was Gervase Wheeler, who came to America from England in the 1840's, had one of his designs published in Downing's last book, and in 1851 brought out his own *Rural Homes,* which was reissued eight times between then and 1869. Many architects more often remembered for things of quite other sorts worked in it. Richard Upjohn, whose Trinity, New York, represents the Gothic Revival at its most "correct," had a line in small country churches of wood that are at least as much Stick Style as they are Gothic. Leopold Eidlitz in several secular commissions forsook the masonry of his churches to produce what the critic Montgomery

112   The Stick Style

Schuyler called "expositions of the mechanical facts of the case" in wood. Even the French-trained Richard Morris Hunt, before the Châteauesque and the Vanderbilts claimed him for their own, resorted to the Stick Style for two or three "cottages" at Newport.

Bibliography references: 4, 10, 18, 57, 114

1. House at San Luis Obispo, California. Circa 1880. (Photo: Richard M. Firestone)
2. Cram House, Middletown, Rhode Island. Dudley Newton, architect, 1871-1872. (The Preservation Society of Newport County. Photo: Robert Meservey)
3. Griswold House, Newport, Rhode Island. Richard Morris Hunt, architect, 1862-1863. (Preservation Society of Newport County. Photo: Robert Meservey)
4. St. Luke's Episcopal Church, Metuchen, New Jersey. 1868. (HABS, Library of Congress. Photo: Jack E. Boucher)

3

The Queen Anne Style

Irregularity of plan and massing and variety of color and texture characterize the Queen Anne Style. Several different wall surfaces may occur in one building; brick for the ground story with shingles or horizontal boards above is a common combination. There may be some half timbering – perhaps only in a gable or two. Upper stories may project beyond those below. Windows are of many forms, straight-topped or round-arched (never pointed-arched); they may be glazed with plate glass or, sometimes in their upper parts only, with small panes set in lead or wooden sash. Bay windows are much employed. Roofs are high and multiple, their ridges meeting at right angles; the round or polygonal turret is a feature of the later phase of the style. Although hipped roofs are seen, the A-roof is the predominant type. Gables, often including a large porch gable, contribute much to the over-all effect and are given many different treatments. Chimneys also are treated as important features, frequently being paneled or otherwise modeled in cut or molded brick. Detail is generally classical and tends to be small in scale.

History: In England the day of Queen Anne dawned in 1868 with a house in Sussex called Leyswood, designed by Richard Norman Shaw, the most successful English architect of the later nineteenth century. For the first phase of the style, at least, the term Queen Anne was an egregious misnomer; "Queen Elizabeth" would have been more accurate. However, it was not the architecture of the stone and brick "prodigy houses" of Elizabeth I's reign, with their modish foreign detail, that Shaw followed in this and later designs, but a rural manner that was still more than half medieval – though too "late" to be classified as Gothic.

From the early seventies Shaw's houses were published in the architectural press, with his own fine perspectives reproduced by the new technique of photolithography, and thus came to be known, admired, and imitated on this side of the Atlantic. Henry Hobson Richardson was the first and greatest of the American architects to work in the "Shavian Manorial" style (as Henry-Russell Hitchcock has called the first phase of Queen Anne). In the Watts Sherman House at Newport, Rhode Island (1874), he followed Shaw very closely indeed, while giving the building a degree of American and even regional character by

3

substituting shingles for tiles as the facing of the upper walls and stone for brick as the material of the walls of the ground story. (Rhode Island was the only one of the original colonies to have building stone on the seaboard.)

The popular success of Queen Anne in America dates from the Philadelphia Centennial Exposition of 1876, at which the British government put up two half-timbered buildings to provide living quarters and offices for the British Executive Commissioner and his staff. The *American Builder,* which recognized that despite the accepted designation they were "essentially Elizabethan in character," said that they were "the most interesting and by far the most conspicuous and costly buildings erected by any foreign Government on the Centennial grounds." After an enthusiastic description, the magazine observed,

"But the chief thing that will strike the observant eye in this style is its wonderful adaptability to this country, not to the towns indeed, but to the land at large.... It is to be hoped that the next millionaire who puts up a cottage at Long Branch will adopt this style, and he will have a house ample enough to entertain a Prince, yet exceedingly cozy, cool

4

in summer, and yet abundantly warm in winter, plain enough, and yet capable of the highest ornamental development."
From our distance we can see that Queen Anne – whatever its practical advantages, actual or imagined – represented a reaction against High Victorian "reality" and a renewed interest in picturesque qualities, while it conjured up a period of the past that was just distant enough to appear rosy in the eyes of an America that had lost so much of its confidence in the future during the financial panic of 1873.

Already by 1876, Norman Shaw himself had moved on from the sixteenth century to the seventeenth for his borrowings and had initiated that second phase of Queen Anne which was sometimes called "free classic." In America in the eighties the Shingle Style drew off much of the talent that might otherwise have gone into Queen Anne; leaders

5

of the profession like Bruce Price and McKim, Mead and White might build row houses in New York that seemed restrained after the High Victorian exuberances of the two preceding decades, but in the suburbs Queen Anne was left to what Montgomery Schuyler in 1883 called the Extreme Left – "a frantic and vociferous mob, who welcome the 'new departure' as the disestablishment of all standards, whether of authority or of reason, and as an emancipation from all restraints, even those of public decency."

Bibliography references: 10, 18, 19, 30, 50, 52, 57, 100, 110

1. Los Angeles Heritage Society, Los Angeles, California. Circa 1890. (Photo: Julius Shulman)
2, 3. Mutual Fire Insurance Company Building, Germantown, Pennsylvania. George T. Pearson, architect, 1884-1885. Demolished 1959. (HABS, Library of Congress. Photo: Theodore F. Dillon)
4, 5. Sagamore Hill, Oyster Bay, New York. Lamb and Rich, architects, 1884-1885. (HABS, Library of Congress. Photo: Jack E. Boucher)
6. House at Calvert, Texas. Circa 1890. (Texas Architecture Survey. Photo: Todd Webb)

1

The Eastlake Style

Most Eastlake buildings would be classifiable as Stick Style or Queen Anne if they were not transmogrified by a distinctive type of ornament. This ornament is largely the product of the chisel, the gouge, and the lathe (and thus fundamentally different from the two-dimensional gingerbread of the scroll saw). Curved brackets are placed wherever curved brackets will go. The posts of porches or verandas, and sometimes the exposed framing members of roofs, often bear a marked resemblance to table legs; rows of spindles – forming openwork friezes or fascias along those same porches or verandas, for example – are much employed. Other borrowings from furniture include knobs of various forms and decorative motifs consisting of circular perforations.

The Eastlake Style

History: Charles Lock Eastlake, son of the painter Sir Charles Eastlake (with whom he is sometimes confused), was an English architect whose buildings are less often remembered than his two books, *A History of the Gothic Revival* and *Hints on Household Taste.* The latter, which is the one that concerns us, was first published in London in 1868. The first American edition appeared in Boston in 1872, and the book became an immediate success on this side of the Atlantic with six more editions in the next eleven years. This was not without its embarrassments for the author. In the preface to the fourth English edition (1878), Eastlake warned readers against supposing that the small woodcuts in the book could serve as models for upholsterers and cabinetmakers without working drawings. "I think it the more necessary to state this," he added, "as I find American tradesmen continually advertising what they are pleased to call 'Eastlake' furniture, with the production of which I have had nothing whatever to do, and for the taste of which I should be very sorry to be considered responsible."

Yet worse was to come. Three years later Eastlake wrote,
"I now find, to my amazement, that there exists on the other side of the Atlantic an 'Eastlake style' of architecture, which, judging from the specimens I have seen illustrated, may be said to burlesque such doctrines of art as I have ventured to maintain. . . . I feel greatly flattered by the popularity which my books have attained in America, but I regret that their author's name should be associated there with a phase of taste in architecture and industrial art with which I can have no real sympathy, and which by all accounts seems to be extravagant and *bizarre.*"

This was printed in 1882 in the *California Architect and Building News,* whose editors had asked whether "the monstrosities denominated 'Eastlake'" had anything in common with "the unique and beautiful designs projected by Charles L. Eastlake, of Leinster Square, London." And it was in California and the West generally that the style persisted longest – down to the late eighties – and reached its most *outré* development in the Eastlake-Second Empire amalgam of so many San Francisco row houses.

Bibliography reference: 63

1. Double house on Twenty-first Street, San Francisco, California. Circa 1880. (Photo: Morley Baer)
2. House on Buchanan Street, San Francisco, California. Circa 1875. (Photo: Morley Baer, from *Here Today*. . . . , published by The Chronicle Publishing Co., San Francisco)
3. Brownlee House, Bonham, Texas. Circa 1885. (Texas Architecture Survey. Photo: Todd Webb)

The Shingle Style

The walls of the upper stories at least, and often of the ground story too, have a uniform covering of shingles; even the posts of verandas and porches may be shingled. Where the ground-story walls are not shingled, they are typically of stone – coursed or random rubble or sometimes fieldstone boulders. Windows are small-paned and often form horizontal bands; a single Palladian window occasionally appears. Roofs may be hipped or gabled or both, intersecting as in the Queen Anne style; the gambrel roof (not a Queen Anne feature) was used quite frequently. Roofs generally are of moderate pitch with broad gable ends; there is a well-defined type of house in which the main front is unified by a single broad gable. Sometimes a roof will sweep down from the ridge without a break to shelter a veranda. Segmental bays and round turrets are not uncommon, and the roofs to dormers sometimes take convex or polygonal forms. The over-all effect is altogether simpler and quieter than in the Queen Anne style, with more horizontal emphasis and much less variety of color and texture.

History: The Shingle Style succeeded Queen Anne as the most up-to-date mode for houses around 1880. (Vincent Scully, its namer and historian, calls a house of 1879 by the architect William Ralph Emerson its "first fully developed monument.") In one way, it may be seen as a development from, and an Americanization of, Queen Anne – an Americanization in intention as well as in effect, for its borrowings from seventeenth-century New England architecture, unsystematic and unscholarly though they normally were, were sufficient to make it (in Hitchcock's words) "to its protagonists already a sort of Colonial Revival." Looked at in another way, as an architecture in which the frame is totally concealed and walls and roof are perceived as a thin skin shaped by the enclosed space, it represented the ultimate reaction against the structuralism of the Stick Style, that High Victorian architecture of skeleton. It was also – and it could be argued that herein lay its real importance – a style that brought a new freedom and openness into the planning of the American house.

The Shingle Style came into being in New England – the house by Emerson was at Mount Desert, Maine – and New England architects were ever among the leaders in its development. Besides Emerson, there were Peabody and Stearns, Arthur Little, and Henry Paston Clark, all of Boston, and John Calvin Stevens of Portland, Maine; the last was something of a specialist in the use of the gambrel roof, and certain of his designs help one to see how the Shingle Style could have been regarded as Colonial. Henry Hobson Richardson (a New Englander by adoption) designed his first Shingle Style house as early as 1880 and, in 1882, what is certainly one of the masterpieces of the style in the Stoughton House at Cambridge. One of his last works was the rather similar Potter House at St. Louis, Missouri (1886).

Among other notable Shingle Style houses in New England are, or were, several by McKim, Mead and White. The largest is Southside, at Newport, designed in 1882; probably the best of those still standing is Edna Villa (the Isaac Bell House) on Bellevue Avenue, Newport, also of 1882. Unhappily, the house in which McKim, Mead and White demonstrated that the Shingle Style had potentialities that few before them had suspected, and none had fully exploited, and which ranked with the Stoughton House as a masterpiece, was demolished by its owner in the early 1960's. This was the Low House at Bristol, Rhode Island. It

3

was designed in 1887, the same year as the Boston Public Library, and with its symmetrical gabled front it was clearly the result of the same quest for discipline – here, however, found without recourse to historical precedent or classical forms.

Outside New England, Lamb and Rich of New York were practitioners of the style and did much work in New Jersey, at Short Hills in particular. Bruce Price, the father of Mrs. Emily Post, was another, and a very prolific one; among his best works were small houses of a most individual character in the socially desirable and sartorially innovatory suburb of Tuxedo Park, New York, for the over-all plan of which he was

4

also responsible. In Philadelphia there was Wilson Eyre. In Chicago there was J. Lyman Silsbee, Frank Lloyd Wright's first employer, while in 1887 John Wellborn Root designed one of the finest nondomestic buildings of the style in Lake View Presbyterian Church. The first (1889) section of Wright's own house in Oak Park is Shingle Style, its design owing more than a little to Bruce Price's Chandler House in Tuxedo Park, which had been published in the magazine *Building* three years earlier.

The Shingle Style was taken to San Francisco in 1886 by Willis Polk. Despite its New England origin it flourished in California. The Hotel del Coronado, near San Diego, built in 1886-1888 to the designs of the brothers James and Merritt Reid, must be the largest Shingle Style building still standing.

Bibliography references: 1, 10, 19, 30, 57, 63

1. House House, Austin, Texas. Frank Freeman, architect, 1891; demolished 1967. (Texas Architecture Survey. Photo: Todd Webb)
2, 3. Potter House, St. Louis, Missouri. Henry Hobson Richardson, architect, 1886-1887. (Photo: Richard Nickel)
4. Joseph House, Middletown, Rhode Island. Clarence S. Luce, architect, 1882-1883. (Preservation Society of Newport County. Photo: Robert Meservey)
5. Bookstaver House, Middletown, Rhode Island. J. D. Johnston, architect, 1885. (Preservation Society of Newport County. Photo: Robert Meservey)

Richardsonian Romanesque

Like all Romanesque, this is a round-arched style. However, most of the buildings of the Richardsonian Romanesque are immediately distinguishable from those of the earlier Romanesque Revival by being wholly or in part of rock-faced masonry, while arches, lintels, and other structural features are often emphasized by being of a different stone from the walls. The resultant sense of weight and massiveness is reinforced by the depth of the window reveals, the breadth of the planes of the roofs, and (in the better examples) a general largeness and simplicity of form.

Straight-topped windows, divided into rectangular lights by stone mullions and transoms, are employed in addition to, and often together with, the arched type; ribbon windows, their arches or lintels supported by colonnettes, occur frequently. In multistory urban buildings – public or commercial – the size of the arched openings, which form arcades behind which from two to four stories may be grouped, often diminishes upward. In porches the Syrian arch is much used.

Steep-gabled wall dormers may be prominent elements in the design. Roof dormers, on the other hand, are usually subordinated to the roofs by being hipped, or even reduced to "eyebrow" form. Square towers are crowned with pyramidal roofs and the characteristic round or polygonal turrets and projecting bays with conical. Chimneys are squat, heavy-set, and very plainly treated – often without as much as projecting caps.

History: Henry Hobson Richardson is generally recognized as one of the three greatest American-born architects, along with Louis Sullivan and Frank Lloyd Wright. He was born in Louisiana in 1838. After graduating from Harvard in 1859 he went to Paris, to become the second American architectural student (after R. M. Hunt) to attend the Ecole des beaux-arts, though the Civil War, by cutting off his allowance from home, prevented his finishing the course. On his return to America in 1865 he set up in practice in New York. Seven years later, in 1872, he won in competition the commission for Trinity Church on Copley Square, Boston. Besides bringing its architect fame and causing him to move his home and office to Boston, Trinity did more than any other single building to change the American concept of Romanesque – to make it Richardsonian.

Richardson's contemporaries were quick to recognize that the central tower of Trinity was modeled upon that of the Old Cathedral at Salamanca. The rest of the church they regarded as Provençal Romanesque, a view of the matter that satisfied the need of the times to find

2

a historical source for every design, however new in spirit. In fact, as Hitchcock has shown, the stylistic mixture in Trinity is not so simple. It can only be called Richardsonian, even if there is more "revival" in it than there is in many of Richardson's later works.

These, numerous and varied in function as they are, were all designed in less than a decade and a half; for Richardson died, aged forty-seven, in 1886. Since his project for Albany Cathedral remained on paper, only one was a church, much smaller than Trinity and of brick (Emmanuel Church, Pittsburgh, 1884-1886). But there were houses and libraries and railroad stations, university buildings, warehouses, office blocks, courthouses, town halls, and a jail. Two major works that demand individual mention in the briefest account, because of their intrinsic quality and the impression they made on other architects, are

3

the Allegheny County Courthouse and Jail in Pittsburgh and the Marshall Field Wholesale Store in Chicago, both designed near the end of his life, in 1884 and 1885 respectively, and finished after his death.

During Richardson's lifetime there was little Richardsonian Romanesque that did not come from the master's own office. McKim, Mead and White's Lovely Lane Methodist Church in Baltimore is almost as remarkable for the early date of its design, 1883, as for its quality. Montgomery Schuyler wrote in 1891,

"While he was living and practising architecture, architects who regarded themselves as in any degree his rivals were naturally loth to introduce in a design dispositions or features or details, of which the suggestion plainly came from him. Since his death has 'extinguished envy' and ended rivalry, the admiration his work excited has been free to express itself either in direct imitation or in the adoption and elaboration of the suggestions his work furnished."

Whether or not Schuyler was right about the cause, the late eighties were certainly the bumper years of the Richardsonian Romanesque. Unhappily, the architects responsible did not all share what Schuyler described as Richardson's "power of disposing masses, his insistence upon largeness and simplicity, his impatience of niggling, his straightforward and virile handling of his tasks, that made his successes brilliant, and even his failures interesting."

The successors to Richardson's own practice, Shepley, Rutan, and Coolidge, did some respectable things in the style before abandoning it for Renaissance – for example, the Lionberger Warehouse in St. Louis, which was an intelligent adaptation of the Marshall Field Store design to a smaller building, and the Shadyside Presbyterian Church in Pittsburgh, which is a smaller and simpler Trinity, Boston (which in 1895 they made so much more Provençal than Richardson had left it by adding the west porch, an elaboration of the porch of St.-Gilles-de-Gard). In 1887 they took the Richardsonian Romanesque to the Far West, for the first buildings of Stanford University.

Pittsburgh, where the Allegheny County Courthouse loomed so large, got rather more than its fair share of Richardsonian Romanesque; much of it was from the hand of Frank E. Alden, who had been sent there by Richardson to supervise the construction of the courthouse in 1885. Farther west, in Chicago, Burnham and Root employed the

style in 1886 for the Rookery, and in the following year Louis Sullivan himself made radical changes in the Auditorium elevations under the influence of the Marshall Field Store. Henry Ives Cobb was another Chicago architect who worked in it, most extensively in the Newberry Library of 1892. To the discomfort of Schuyler, it was very popular for residential work in that city. Farther west again, Minneapolis has Pillsbury Hall at the University of Minnesota, designed in 1887 nominally by Leroy Buffington (best remembered for his attempt to patent the skyscraper) but actually by Harvey Ellis, which has been described as "a veritable catalogue of Richardsonian forms"; then there is the imitation of the Allegheny County Courthouse in the Hennepin County

Courthouse and Minneapolis City Hall, begun in 1888 to the designs of Long and Kees.

It was in 1888, also, that the Allegheny Courthouse supplied rather more – or perhaps less – than inspiration for the first Los Angeles County Courthouse, by Curlett, Cuthbertson, and Eisen. The historian of California's nineteenth-century architecture, Harold Kirker, describes this as "so clumsy a theft that one can only conclude that the architects had not even the good sense to make an accurate copy." The astonishing results that the Richardsonian Romanesque could produce in the West are exemplified by the California State Bank at Sacramento, designed by Curlett and Cuthbertson in 1890, which Mr. Kirker shows us in an old photograph in the same book. In the Northwest, downtown Seattle still has a notable display of the style on and around Pioneer Square, dating from the rebuilding after the fire of 1889; the leading architect here was Elmer H. Fisher, whose Pioneer Building is one of the numerous imitations of Burnham and Root's Rookery.

Bibliography references: 2, 7, 10, 18, 20, 30, 52, 62, 63, 74, 95, 115

1. Cheney Building, Hartford, Connecticut. Henry Hobson Richardson, architect, 1875-1876. (Photo: Author)
2. Ayer House, Chicago, Illinois. Burnham and Root, architects, 1885; demolished 1966. (HABS, Library of Congress, Photo: Harold Allen)
3. Pioneer Building, Seattle, Washington. Elmer H. Fisher, architect, 1890. (Photo: Richard S. Alden)
4. The Rookery, Chicago, Illinois. Burnham and Root, architects, 1886. (Photo: Cervin Robinson)
5. Shadyside Presbyterian Church, Pittsburgh, Pennsylvania. Shepley, Rutan, and Coolidge, architects, 1888-1890. (Photo: Harold E. Dickson)

Châteauesque

Châteauesque buildings, always of masonry construction (stone or brick or both), have asymmetrical plans and silhouettes with high, steep-sided hipped roofs rising to a ridge or to a flat top; the roofs in either case are surmounted by metal railings or openwork metal cresting (rather than the solid curb or Second Empire roofs). Round turrets, or *tourelles,* corbeled out from the walls at second-floor level are favorite features; these have conical "candle-snuffer" roofs which contribute much to the general liveliness of the silhouette, as do also the tall and often fancifully treated chimneys. Wall dormers are universal; they have high, pinnacled gables, sometimes incorporating stone tracery, or pediments of steeper pitch than the classical norm. Below the roof, the windows are the features by which the style is most readily identified. They fall into two main types, being either (1) linteled or (2) arched with the kind of arch called (descriptively enough) the basket-handle arch. In both types the openings are

crossed by masonry mullions and transoms, forming what the French call *croisettes*. The basket-handle arch is often used for doorways too, though when the architect was aiming at a "later" effect there may be a porch with a semicircular arch and flanking pilasters. In some designs the detail is predominantly Gothic, with such features as hoodmolds and traceried parapets, in others it is predominantly Renaissance, with pilasters and balustrades, while in others again the Gothic and Renaissance elements are quite evenly mixed.

History: This is most often called the Francis I style. It certainly owes more, on the whole, to the architecture of the reign of that French king (1515-1547), when Italian Renaissance ideas and classical forms combined with the native Gothic tradition to produce a style that is no less distinctive for being "transitional," than the Queen Anne Style owes to that of 1702-1714 in England. However, it so often contains a generous admixture of earlier, fifteenth-century elements – in some cases, indeed, they become the dominant ones – that the term Châteauesque (an ingenious coinage of Bainbridge Bunting) is surely to be preferred.

France had her own revival of the *style François I* in the second quarter of the nineteenth century, and the first American château was designed by an architect of Danish birth who had studied and worked in Paris before settling in New York in 1848. His name was Detlef Lienau, and his client was the railroad magnate LeGrand Lockwood, whose million-dollar mansion at South Norwalk, Connecticut, was built in 1864-1868. This, however, was the single swallow that did not make the summer, which came in fifteen years later when Richard Morris Hunt designed William Kissam Vanderbilt's house on Fifth Avenue, New York. Hunt was the first American architect to study at the École des beaux-arts, and his eclecticism was of the most ambitious kind. The W. K. Vanderbilt house was described by Montgomery Schuyler as "an attempt to summarize in one building the history of a most active and fruitful century in the history of architecture, which included the late Gothic of the fifteenth century and the early Renaissance of the sixteenth, and spanned the distance from the minute and complicated modelling of the Palais de Justice at Rouen and the Hôtel Cluny at Paris, to the romantic classicism of the great châteaux of the Loire."

Hunt remained the leader of the movement, and Vanderbilts were its most munificent patrons. It reached its culmination in the enormous Biltmore, near Asheville, North Carolina, which Hunt built for George Washington Vanderbilt in 1890-1895. This is a château in size and setting as well as in style; Hunt's earlier Ochre Court at Newport, Rhode Island, built for Ogden Goelet in 1885-1889, lacks only the setting. Other leading architects who housed Vanderbilts in châteaux were Hunt's former pupil George B. Post, who began one on Fifth Avenue for Cornelius Vanderbilt II as early as 1880, and (inevitably) Stanford White, who completed one for W. K. Vanderbilt, Jr., next door to his father's, as late as 1905.

The Châteauesque, whose special piquancy resulted from the adroit mixing of Renaissance and Late Gothic details, was rather tricky for any but the *cordons bleus* of the profession. By the eighties architects were more chary of taking liberties with the styles than they had been in the High Victorian decades. Queen Anne was easier to do, more appropriate for normal-size jobs, and more democratic in its associations. However, in the Gresham House at Galveston, Texas, Nicholas J. Clayton combined salient features of the style and details from several others with a more than High Victorian confidence. Countless houses were given something of a château air with high roofs, wall dormers, and ornamental cresting, when other features did little or nothing to support the effect. And the conical-roofed turret was hospitably received into both the Queen Anne and the Shingle styles.

Bibliography references: 1, 7, 18, 52

1. Kimball House, Chicago, Illinois. Solon Spencer Beman, architect, 1890-1892. (HABS, Library of Congress. Photo: Harold Allen)
2. Borden House, Chicago, Illinois. Richard Morris Hunt, architect, 1884; demolished 1960. (Photo: Richard Nickel)
3. Gresham House (The Bishop's Palace), Galveston, Texas. Nicholas J. Clayton, architect, 1888-1892. (Texas Architecture Survey. Photo: Todd Webb)

4: Styles That Reached Their Zenith in 1890-1915

The division between modernism, meaning complete or relative freedom from forms culled from styles of the past, and so-called traditionalism, or historical eclecticism, becomes a feature of the architectural scene – modernism being represented by the Commercial Style, the Sullivanesque, the Prairie Style, the Western Stick Style, and the Bungaloid. In historical eclecticism the trend was toward academicism and the "correct"; such freedoms as the bolder spirits among the eclectics permitted themselves are usually less noticeable than their general conformism.

Beaux-Arts Classicism

Coupled columns are among the commonest features of Beaux-Arts Classicism; their presence amounts to presumptive evidence that a building is of this style. Monumental flights of steps are also characteristic. Arched and linteled openings, often set between columns or pilasters, may appear together in the same elevation. Figure sculpture, in the round or in relief, appears more frequently than in any of the other classical styles and may be used – as almost never in the others – to enliven the skyline. The planning and massing of buildings are strictly and sometimes elaborately symmetrical, with clearly articulated parts; in large buildings a five-part composition, with a climactic central mass dominating the wings and their terminal features, is typical. Fronts may be much broken into advancing and receding planes, and a general tendency to multiply re-entrant angles sometimes affects even the treatment of the quoins.

1

Beaux-Arts Classicism

History: In the nineteenth century the Ecole des beaux-arts, in Paris, had an unrivaled reputation among schools of architecture. The first American to attend it was Richard Morris Hunt; the second was Henry Hobson Richardson (who did not complete the course for financial reasons). By the end of the century the architectural profession in America was dominated by men who had followed their example.

The highest distinction within the reach of the student at the Ecole was the winning of the Grand Prix de Rome. This prize, which had been instituted in 1717, sent its winner to Rome for three more years of study and assured him of public commissions after his return to France. It was awarded on the basis of a single project designated each year by the school authorities. The project was invariably of a grandiose nature; there was no specific site, and the program was

written in those sonorous generalities to which the French language so readily lends itself. In the competition, which was judged by a jury, there were two requisites for success: first, a demonstration of expertise in the approved convention of planning, which demanded clear articulation of functions and a hierarchy of major and minor axes and cross axes; second, skillfully executed elevational drawings with plenty to look at in them. It was in the provision of the latter that the competitor of above-average talent (though not necessarily architectural talent) had an edge over his rivals, with the result that what might be called classical pictorialism became the end product of Beaux-Arts training.

In the absence of other signs, such as borrowings from certain admired models of the French seventeenth and eighteenth centuries or

3

combinations of columns and arches that were the result of a theory that the Greek and Roman structural systems should be synthesized, this pictorialism is what distinguishes Beaux-Arts Classicism from the other classical styles of its time. An instructive comparison may be made between two versions of the Mausoleum at Halicarnassus, designed within five years of each other; namely, the Allegheny County Soldiers and Sailors Memorial in Pittsburgh (Palmer and Hornbostel, completed in 1908), which with its translation of the Greek model into Roman architectural terms represents Beaux-Arts Classicism at its most confident, and the Temple of the Scottish Rite in Washington (John Russell Pope, 1910-1916), which is a canonical example of the Neo-Classical Revival.

Beaux-Arts Classicism is the style of many well-known public and quasi-public buildings in the United States, from libraries (such as the New York Public Library, Carrère and Hastings, 1895-1902) to railroad stations (such as the New York Grand Central Terminal, Warren and Wetmore, 1903-1913). But it was in the plaster architecture of the exhibitions that the style really came into its own. One of the best and boldest examples was the focal Administration Building of the 1893 Columbian Exposition in Chicago, designed by Richard Morris Hunt, who upon a ground story that combined arches and columns in the Roman manner placed a colonnaded Greek upper story, with flourishes of statuary at the angles, and crowned the whole tall structure with a version of the dome of Florence Cathedral. Among the many manifestations of Beaux-Arts Classicism in the exhibitions of the early years of the twentieth century, four may be singled out for mention: the Electric Tower at the Pan-American Exposition, Buffalo (John Galen Howard, 1901); the Festival Hall and Cascades at the Louisiana Purchase Exposition, St. Louis (Cass Gilbert and E. L. Masqueray, 1904); the Tower of Jewels at the San Francisco Panama-Pacific International Exhibition (Carrère and Hastings, 1915); and the Palace of Fine Arts at the same exhibition, by Bernard Maybeck. The last of these, a piece of architectural scenery of real originality and power if not of the most permanent materials, was recently demolished to make way for a concrete reproduction of itself.

Bibliography references: 5, 7, 10, 18, 20, 28

1. Riverside County Courthouse, Riverside, California. Burnham and Bliesner, architect, 1903. (Photo: Author)
2. Metropolitan Museum of Art, New York. Richard Morris Hunt, architect, 1895. (Metropolitan Museum of Art)
3. Memorial Hall, Philadelphia, Pennsylvania. Herman J. Schwarzman, architect, 1875-1876. (Photo: John R. Wells)

The Second Renaissance Revival

Only general guidelines can be laid down for distinguishing buildings of this from those of the earlier Renaissance Revival. Usually they are larger, both absolutely and in scale. Stone, or even marble, takes the place of stucco as a facing material. The imitative use of cast iron for classical ornament and detailing, so common in the earlier North Italian mode, was a thing of the past by the time the Second Renaissance Revival was launched. The range of Italian models was much increased – though this, of course, can hardly be appreciated except in an over-all view.

History: Much as Neo-Classicism began as a movement to discipline the general classical tradition after the "licentious" and "capricious" Baroque age, the Second Renaissance Revival was in the first place the result of a felt need for simplicity and order in reaction to the very different qualities admired in the High Victorian period. The revival opened with the Villard Houses in New York, whose design came from the office of McKim, Mead and White in 1883. The actual designer, and the man responsible for the choice of style, was Joseph Morrill Wells, a young architect who was recognized by all who knew him as having exceptional talent, but who died seven years later at the age of thirty-

2

six. Wells took as model the late-fourteenth-century Cancelleria Palace in Rome. That is to say, he adopted its rusticated ground story and its four types of window. However, he omitted the two pilaster orders of the Cancelleria, thus making his façades simpler and flatter – and reversing the whole tendency of Italianate design.

The most famous building of the Second Renaissance Revival is the Boston Public Library, built to the designs of McKim, Mead and White in 1888-1892. Here the archetype for the arcaded front was an earlier *quattrocento* building, according to McKim, who, when he was taxed with having imitated a famous Parisian library built forty years before,

4

said that it had been inspired by the side elevations of Alberti's church of San Francesco at Rimini.

For the New York Herald, McKim, Mead and White designed a much elongated version of the Loggia del Consiglio at Verona; their University Club in New York, built in the last year of the century, is again *quattrocento,* but Florentine. However, later phases of the Renaissance were also laid under contribution. For the prodigious Cornelius Vanderbilt house at Newport, Rhode Island, called The Breakers,

The Second Renaissance Revival

Richard Morris Hunt in 1892 turned to sixteenth-century Genoa, as did Stanford White for the Washington Club in Washington, D.C., in 1902; Cass Gilbert reproduced the dome of St. Peter's on his Minnesota Capitol; in 1909 John Russell Pope modeled the Hitt House in Washington on the Queen's House at Greenwich, designed by Inigo Jones in the early seventeenth century but still Renaissance in character. The Boston Public Library had belated progeny in the public libraries of San Francisco (George Kelham, 1915) and Detroit (Cass Gilbert, 1921). The revival dragged on, its vitality diminishing as its learning increased, down to the 1930's, a late example showing the somewhat negative virtues it retained being John Russell Pope's Brazilian Embassy of 1931 in Washington, an emasculated version of Peruzzi's Massimi Palace in Rome.

Bibliography references: 1, 5, 7, 10, 18, 20, 38, 53

1. City Hall, Portland, Oregon. Whidden and Lewis, architects, 1892-1895. (Photo: Author)
2. Detroit Public Library, Detroit, Michigan. Cass Gilbert, architect, 1918-1921. (Department of Reports and Information, City of Detroit)
3. The Breakers, Newport, Rhode Island. Richard Morris Hunt, architect, 1892-1895. (Preservation Society of Newport County. Photo: Robert Meservey)
4. The Racquet and Tennis Club, New York. McKim, Mead and White, architects, 1916-1918. (HABS, Library of Congress. Photo: Jack E. Boucher)

The Georgian Revival

The architects of the Georgian Revival worked in two distinct modes. One of them was the Neo-Adamesque, drawing its inspiration from the dominant style of the Federal Period, described earlier in this book; its products tend to be more elaborate and also larger than those of the Adam Style proper. The other is the Neo-Colonial, with its main source in Georgian Colonial architecture, although it also draws on English architecture of the same period. Neo-Colonial buildings are strictly rectangular in plan, with a minimum of minor projections, and have strictly symmetrical façades. Roofs are hipped, double-pitched, or of gambrel form; their eaves are detailed as classical cornices. A hipped roof is often topped with a flat deck, with a surrounding railing or balustrade; sometimes there is a central cupola. Chimneys are placed so as to contribute to the over-all symmetry. The central part of a façade may project slightly and be crowned with a pediment, with or

without supporting pilasters; more rarely, a portico with freestanding columns may form the central feature. Doorways have fanlights and are often set in tabernacle frames. The standard form of window in secular buildings is rectangular with double-hung sash; the Palladian window is often used as a focal incident. Churches have arched windows; the commonest type of steeple has a square tower with a superstructure built up in several stages, the upper ones octagonal in plan, and terminating in a spire.

History: The building that from the viewpoint of history may be seen as the first harbinger of the Georgian Revival was the Arlington Street Church in Boston, built to the design of Arthur D. Gilman in 1859-1861. It is modeled on James Gibbs's church of St. Martin-in-the-Fields in London, built in 1722-1726, which was a favorite model of church builders in colonial times. Post-bellum but still remarkably early was a row of four houses (two of which remain) on Commonwealth Avenue, Boston, designed by Snell and Gregerson in 1866, with bowed fronts in Boston's Beacon Hill tradition combined with the blocked window architraves of English Palladianism. The Georgian Revival as a movement started twenty years later, with two houses by McKim, Mead and White that exemplified what were to be its two principal manners. The Taylor House of 1885-1886 at Newport, Rhode Island, was in the Georgian Colonial manner, wood-framed and clapboarded; it was the progenitor of that long line of suburban houses of which the so-called "Williamsburg-style" boxes of today's subdivisions are the dwarfish and degenerate descendants. The Cochrane House at 257 Commonwealth Avenue, Boston, built in 1886, is except for its doorway in the Adam Style. As a predominantly brick style this did not present the same problems where fire ordinances were concerned and so became the preferred mode for urban buildings.

The Georgian Revival was coeval with the Second Renaissance Revival, was motivated by the same desire to restore order to the architectural scene, and was initiated by the same firm of architects, who maintained their leadership of it for the remaining years of the century. In 1890, McKim, Mead and White built three more Neo-Adamesque houses in Boston, and two years later they gave Chicago a very grand specimen of the style in the Lathrop House; their Germantown Cricket

3

Club of 1890 is notable as an example of brick colonialism of the simpler kind; their porticoed Crossways at Newport, designed for Stuyvesant Fish in 1898, might be taken for a colonial house of the less simple, Palladian kind, if colonial houses had ever been more than half its size. Another firm in the van of the movement was Little and Browne of Boston. Arthur Little had published a serious study of the colonial interior as early as 1878 – the year after that in which McKim, Mead and White made a famous trip along the New England coast in search of colonial buildings. In his own house on Bay State Road in Boston, built in 1890, he interpreted the style of Charles Bulfinch with originality and finesse; during the subsequent decade he designed several houses in the same city that are more directly inspired by Adam's own work in England.

4

Charles A. Platt, William A. Delano, and Chester H. Aldrich are among the other architects whose work would demand discussion in an extended account of the Georgian Revival in America, for which this is not the place. It is still difficult to feel much enthusiasm for its twentieth-century manifestations, numerous and varied (at least superficially) though they are. No architect working in it had the genius of Sir Edwin Lutyens in England. With a few exceptions – one being St. Martin-in-the-Fields, copied by Coolidge and Shattuck for All Souls Unitarian Church, Washington, in 1924 – its historical prototypes were of domestic scale, even when their functions were not strictly domestic; this immediately presented a difficulty when many twentieth-century building types were concerned. (In one domestic type, the apartment block, the accepted "solution" was to concentrate the Georgian detail at top and

5

bottom and leave the middle stories to look after themselves.) To scale down the Doric order of the Parthenon by a fifth, as Strickland did for the Philadelphia Custom House, is one thing; to enlarge the tower of Independence Hall by twice as much is quite another. Many of the public and educational buildings of the Georgian Revival have a special sort of unreality that is increased rather than diminished by the "correctness" of their detail. Yet it should be acknowledged that the Neo-Adamesque façades that went up in such numbers along the streets of New York and other cities in the 1920's constitute the last consistent street architecture that America has had.

Bibliography references: 5, 7, 10, 52, 57, 63

1. Dudley Newton House, Newport, Rhode Island. Dudley Newton, architect, 1897. (Preservation Society of Newport County. Photo: Robert Meservey)
2. All Souls Unitarian Church, Washington, D.C. Coolidge and Shattuck, architects, 1924. (Photo: J. Alexander)
3. Germantown Cricket Club, Germantown, Pennsylvania. McKim, Mead and White, architects, 1890. (Photo: Robert Wells)
4. Little House, Boston, Massachusetts. Arthur Little, architect, 1890. (Photo: Bainbridge Bunting)
5. Lathrop House, Chicago, Illinois. McKim, Mead and White, architects, 1892. (HABS, Library of Congress. Photo: Harold Allen)

The Neo-Classical Revival

Buildings of the Neo-Classical Revival are generally larger than those of the nineteenth-century Greek Revival and always simpler in effect than those of Beaux-Arts Classicism. They show none of the tendency to multiply angles and projections that marks the latter style; broad expanses of plain wall surface are common; roof lines, when not level, are quiet, and unbroken by sculptural incidents. The Greek orders are employed much more often than the Roman, and in keeping with this windows and doorways are linteled rather than arched; pedimented porticoes are frequent features. Coupled columns are not used.

History: The architects of what in the first quarter of our century was often referred to as the American Renaissance and is now less politely called the Academic Reaction – that is, the movement that began in the mid-1880's with the Second Renaissance Revival – were cosmopolitans who believed that thanks to them American architecture was at last taking its place with the architecture of the older countries of the Western world. Ironically, in the Neo-Classical Revival they actually produced something that in the light of history is seen to be peculiarly American.

Not that the individual buildings of the Neo-Classical Revival, for all that some of them resemble the buildings of the American Greek Revival more closely than those of classical antiquity, are American in the sense in which Stick Style buildings, say, or many of the houses of the Second Empire Style, are American. It is the revival in its totality that has no parallel on the other side of the Atlantic. There, around 1900, the Europeans who had been trained at the Ecole des beaux-arts with so many of the leaders of the revival were experimenting with the Art Nouveau, while in England the age of Edwardian Baroque and "Wrenaissance" was about to begin. Nowhere outside the United States were the classical orders to be drawn up in so many parade formations – before their final disbandment, as it proved. Nowhere else were fine materials to be so lavishly employed; one would not be surprised to be told that more marble was used in building in the United States in the years 1900-1917 than was used in the Roman Empire during its entire history.

Exhibitions played an important part in bringing in the Neo-Classical Revival. At the Columbian Exposition of 1893 it was Charles B. Atwood's

Fine Arts Building (reconstructed as the Museum of Science and Industry) that, despite the fact that its design was based on a Prix-de-Rome project of thirty-six years before, foreshadowed the quieter shape of things to come. Then at the first major exhibition of the twentieth century, the Pan-American at Buffalo in 1901, George Cary's New York State Building was a standing reproof in the sternest Greek Doric of the exuberance of the Beaux-Arts Classicism around it. By the end of the decade New York City had the largest and one of the finest buildings of the Neo-Classical Revival in Pennsylvania Station, by McKim, Mead and White. Here two versions of the central hall of the Baths of Caracalla (one of them in steel and glass) were screened from the street by Doric elevations that were Roman in detail but Greek in spirit.

The Neo-Classical Revival

The firm of McKim, Mead and White set the pace of the Neo-Classical Revival, as of the Second Renaissance Revival, at least until America's entry into the Great War. Its Greek designs were as accomplished as its Roman, if no more inspired. The McKinley Memorial of 1917 at Niles, Ohio, is a fair example, for all that its rather delicate Doric order was criticized as inappropriate in a monument to a politician of William

McKinley's character. On the other hand, there has been general agreement on the suitability of the massive and solemn Doric employed by Henry Bacon to commemorate another, greater president; indeed, the Lincoln Memorial in Washington (completed in 1917) has been so generally praised, despite the fact that it "might almost have been designed in Paris in the 1780's" (as Hitchcock has written), that it poses the problem of the relationship between quality and "modernity" with exceptional clarity.

Another peripteral building of the second decade of the century in Washington is the Masonic Temple of the Scottish Rite (1910-1916), modeled on the Mausoleum at Halicarnassus, which brought fame to John Russell Pope. The tradition of Ionic museums, founded by the great Prussian architect Schinkel in the early nineteenth century, was revived in this decade by McKim, Mead and White in the Minneapolis Institute of Arts (1912) and carried on by Hubbell and Benes in the Cleveland Museum of Art (1916); local government was Neo-Classically provided for in the Municipal Buildings at Springfield, Massachusetts (Pell and Corbett, 1913), the law in the New York County Court House (Guy Lowell, 1912) and Shelby County Court House, Memphis, Tennessee (Hale and Rogers, 1907), higher education in the broad acres of the Massachusetts Institute of Technology (Welles Bosworth, 1912).

To list buildings of the Neo-Classical Revival from the between-wars period would be a profitless task; many are too big to be overlooked anyhow. Washington has more than its fair share of them, and John Russell Pope designed more than his fair share of those in Washington; his last work was the National Gallery (1938).

Bibliography references: 5, 7, 10, 12, 20

1. Cleveland Museum of Art, Cleveland, Ohio. Hubbell and Benes, architects, 1917. (Cleveland Museum of Art. Photo: Martin Linsey)
2. The Minneapolis Institute of Arts, Minneapolis, Minnesota. McKim, Mead and White, architects, 1912. (Minneapolis Institute of Arts)
3. Pennsylvania Station, New York. McKim, Mead and White, architects, 1906-1910. (HABS, Library of Congress. Photo: Cervin Robinson)
4. United States National Bank, Portland, Oregon. A. E. Doyle, architect, 1916. (Photo: Author)

The Late Gothic Revival

Late Gothic Revival buildings are quieter and "smoother" in design than those of the High Victorian Gothic. Silhouettes are simpler, polychromy is rare (and much less obtrusive when present), and top-heavy effects and calculated clashes of scale are no longer employed. Italian Gothic, a favorite source with the High Victorians, is little drawn upon, and although there may be some mixing of English and French Gothic motifs, the character of any single building is generally quite definitely English *or* French. The French Flamboyant (avoided by the High Victorians as "late" and decadent) is sometimes imitated, and the English Perpendicular comes back into favor. Perpendicular was the chief source of forms for the Early Gothic Revival too, but there is rarely any difficulty in distinguishing between the products of the two periods, even when it comes to churches. Late Gothic Revival churches are substantially built of masonry – stone when it was practicable – and never of wood imitating masonry; tracery is of stone, and many churches are vaulted in masonry or in tile (as none of those of the Early Revival are); the craftsmanship is generally superior, and the detail is more varied even in a single building (the architects of the Early Revival having been content for the most part to use two or three standard moldings and a single pattern of tracery throughout any one design). In commercial buildings the Gothic detail is most often of terra cotta.

History: The building whose place in the history of the Late Gothic Revival corresponds to that of the Villard Houses in the Second Renaissance Revival is the church of All Saints, Ashmont, outside Boston. Its architects were nominally Cram and Wentworth. However, a talented young draftsman who had joined the office two years before worked on the design, which thus became the first joint work of the two architects who were to be the pacesetters of the movement, Ralph Adams Cram and Bertram Grosvenor Goodhue. Cram and Goodhue were formally partners from 1895 until 1913, when Goodhue left the firm, which since Wentworth's death in 1899 had been known as Cram, Goodhue and Ferguson. (Wentworth and Ferguson were businessmen rather than designers.)

As he relates in his autobiography, Cram "evolved a theory" that Gothic architecture "had not suffered a natural death at the beginning of the sixteenth century, but had been most untimely cut off by the synchronizing of the Classical Renaissance and the Protestant Revolution." The thing to do, therefore, was "to take up English Gothic at the point where it was cut off during the reign of Henry VIII and go on from that point, developing the style England had made her own, and along what might be assumed to be logical lines, with due regard to the changing conditions of contemporary culture." So the Late Gothic Revival went back to the English Perpendicular style, which had been the main source of the Early Gothic Revival too, with the idea (which was not a part of the philosophy of the early revival) that the architect should develop it into something new. To do this, it was necessary that the architect should, in a favorite cliché of the time, "make the style his own" – a feat that in the opinion of most critics was accomplished more frequently by certain English architects than by their American colleagues.

In 1903, Cram and Ferguson had their first major success when they won a limited competition for the rebuilding of the United States Military Academy at West Point, against strong classical opposition, with designs in an appropriately militarized version of Perpendicular. The design accepted in 1906 for the rebuilding of St. Thomas' Church, New York, was also Perpendicular; then Cram had second thoughts, and the building as it stands is French Flamboyant. In the following year, 1907, Cram turned to earlier French models when commissioned to complete the Cathedral of St. John the Divine, New York – and to the earliest English Gothic for Calvary Church in Pittsburgh. In church architecture at least, any intention of developing a new style soon gave way to a catholic eclecticism – "synthetic" and productive of a certain piquancy in some instances, such as Goodhue's First Baptist Church in Pittsburgh (1912), in which a generally Perpendicular design is Frenchified with steep roofs and a flèche, but academic and quite archaeological in others, such as the French Gothic Lady Chapel of St. Patrick's Cathedral, New York, designed by Charles T. Matthews.

The Late Gothic Revival flourished in two other fields beside the ecclesiastical – the educational and the commercial. "Collegiate Gothic" was introduced at Bryn Mawr in the early nineties by Cope and Stewardson, who in 1896 carried it to the campus on which it was to flourish as nowhere else, that of Princeton University. The supervising architect at Princeton from 1909 until 1931 was none other than Cram, who designed the Graduate School there, completed in 1913; this was immediately joined by other Late Perpendicular buildings by Day and Klauder. Yale soon followed Princeton's example with the aid of James Gamble Rogers, who designed the Harkness Quadrangle in 1917; his irresistibly scenic Harkness Memorial Tower is exceptional among Gothic buildings for higher education in not being wholly English in inspiration. Duke University, at Durham, North Carolina, and the University of

176 The Late Gothic Revival

3

Chicago also opted for Gothic; at Duke the architect of the Men's Campus was Horace Trumbauer, while the Rockefeller Memorial Chapel of the University of Chicago was one of Goodhue's last works, completed after his death. In the educational field Late Gothic Revival architecture culminated, in the literal sense of the word, in the University of Pittsburgh's skyscraping Cathedral of Learning, designed by Charles Zeller Klauder in 1925.

Some of the steel-frame skyscrapers of the 1890's were given unobtrusive Gothic ornament. In the fifty-two-story Woolworth Building, New York, completed in 1913, Cass Gilbert not only employed Gothic ornament of a more elaborate (French) type but Gothicized the total form of the building, which is rather like a Gothic church seen in one of those distorting mirrors which exaggerate the vertical dimension. Of the later Gothic skyscrapers that admiration of Cass Gilbert's masterpiece led to, the Tribune Tower in Chicago, built to the design of Hood and Howells in 1923-1925, is the best known and conceivably the best – though scarcely in the same class as the Woolworth Building. The *succès d'estime* enjoyed by the design that gained the Finnish architect Eliel Saarinen second premium in the Chicago Tribune competition resulted in the adoption for skyscrapers of a kind of stripped Gothic, free of the archaeologizing detail of Hood's design, that soon merged into the Modernistic of the later twenties.

As its verticality suggested Gothic as suitable for skyscrapers, so its large window areas suggested it for other commercial buildings – and even, on occasion, for industrial ones. In such cases the Gothic touches are usually quite frankly applied as "styling" to a design whose over-all character has been determined by other factors, functional or economic. But that is not to say that they may not be skillfully applied, as in the works of George C. Nimmons, for example, a Chicago architect much employed by Sears, Roebuck and Company.

Bibliography references: 5, 7, 20, 23, 39, 47

1. Calvary Episcopal Church, Pittsburgh, Pennsylvania. Ralph Adams Cram, architect, 1907. (Calvary Episcopal Church)
2. Chapel, Duke University, Durham, North Carolina. Horace Trumbauer, architect, 1932. (Library of Congress. Photo: Frances Benjamin Johnston)
3. High School, Evanston, Illinois. Perkins, Fellows and Hamilton, architects, 1926. (Photo: Chicago Architectural Photo. Co.)

The Jacobethan Revival

Windows, gables, and chimneys are of distinctive forms. Windows are rectangular and are divided into rectangular lights by stone mullions; the larger windows, which may be very large, have stone transoms too. Bay windows are frequent features. Gables, which rise above the roof, either are of a steep-sided triangular form or have a silhouette composed of segmental curves and straight lines in combination. (The latter type of gable is a feature shared with the Mission Style, which is quite different in other respects, however.) Roofs are ridged, or flat and parapeted, or hipped; in large buildings, towers and turrets may be crowned with

1

curvilinear roofs ("shapes," as they were formerly called). Chimneys are tall, with a separate shaft for each flue; the shafts are grouped in stacks or, more typically, lined up in rows, with each shaft set diagonally to its neighbors. Doorways, usually round-arched, may be enclosed within tabernacle frames; the use of classical forms elsewhere is minimal as a rule. Brick and stone are the favorite materials – brick for the walls and stone for window frames, parapets, quoins, and ornament. A type of ornament peculiar to the style is strapwork, which consists of flat scrollwork that somewhat resembles – as the name implies – leather straps.

History: The adjective "Jacobethan" is compounded from Jacobean and Elizabethan. It appeared in print for the first time, to the present author's knowledge, rather more than thirty years ago in a poem by John Betjeman. There it was used within quotation marks to describe a four-poster bed (of twentieth-century manufacture) in an English middle-class suburban home. In the 1950's it was taken up for a more serious purpose by Henry-Russell Hitchcock, who removed the quotation marks and added the noun Revival to denote the architectural phenomenon under discussion. Hitchcock himself admitted that this was not really a revival in the full sense of the term, as was the Gothic Revival, for example; moreover, nobody calls English architecture of the reigns of Elizabeth I and James I, which supplied its models, Jacobethan. For all that, it seems best to retain the noun to emphasize the derivative nature of the style.

When a few instances of the imitation of Elizabethan and Jacobean forms in the eighteenth century have been left out of account because of the special attendant circumstances – including the need to harmonize the design with actual work of the earlier period – the Jacobethan Revival may be said to have been born in England around 1830; while still of tender years it received official recognition of a singular kind when in 1835 the terms of the competition for the new Houses of Parliament stated that designs were to be "Gothic or Elizabethan" – though, as everyone knows, Gothic won the day. In a book published in 1833, the architect Francis Goodwin, employing a name for the style that Sir Charles Barry, the architect successful in the Houses of Parliament competition, also favored, described the attractions of "the

2

modern Anglo-Italian" as a style that "tolerates many freedoms" and "can dispense with strictness as to detail," concluding that "it offers a certain unconstricted liveliness" which "is far from being out of place where cheerfulness is the quality principally aimed at."

In America, qualified approval was given to the Jacobethan Revival by Andrew Jackson Downing (who incidentally seems not to have been altogether certain whether most of Queen Elizabeth's reign fell in the sixteenth century or in the seventeenth). In Downing's view, "the florid Elizabethan style" was "a very dangerous one in the hands of any one but an architect of profound taste." Yet he thought that "in some of its simpler forms" the Elizabethan might be "adopted for country residences here in picturesque situations with a quaint and happy effect";

in proof, he illustrated a curly-gabled "Mansion in the Elizabethan Style" near Yonkers.

Jacobethan designs are included in other mid-century books, beside Downing's. Actual buildings in the style from the period are few and far between and have to be sought out. Any Jacobethan building encountered by chance is likely to have been built considerably later – most probably, since 1890. By that year the style could be regarded as a "cheerful" alternative to the solemnities of the Academic Reaction, and soon there would be the books of J. A. Gotch and other English architect-antiquaries to facilitate that "strictness as to detail" which the spirit of the times (no longer Goodwin's) demanded even in buildings in which cheerfulness was aimed at. Although most Jacobethan designs may have been for houses, it was on educational architecture that the style had its greatest impact proportionally. What must surely be the showiest productions of the whole revival are the buildings at the University of Pennsylvania designed from 1895 on by Cope and Stewardson,

3

the Collegiate Gothic experts. More typical, and at least as worthy of critical consideration, is the series of schools at St. Louis, Missouri, for which William B. Ittner was the architect.

Bibliography references: 5, 7, 10, 75, 83

1. University Club, Portland, Oregon. Morris H. Whitehouse and J. André Fouilhoux, architects, 1912. (Photo: Author)
2. Dormitories, University of Pennsylvania, Philadelphia, Pennsylvania. Walter Cope and John Stewardson, architects, 1895. (Photo: Robert Wells)
3. Cranbrook, Bloomfield Hills, Michigan. Albert Kahn, architect, 1909. (Photo: Author)

The Commercial Style

Commercial Style buildings are of five to sixteen stories with straight fronts, or slight central projections at most, flat roofs, and level skylines. The character of their façades derives from the fenestration, to which any ornament – often there is none – is altogether subordinate. The pattern is often entirely regular; such grouping of windows as there may be usually has to be looked for to be seen. The windows themselves are rectangular (or, in bearing-wall structures, sometimes segmental-headed), very large, and variously divided; a common type, known as the

Chicago window, has a broad central light of plate glass, fixed, and narrow side lights with opening sash; bay windows are often employed. The total area of glass normally exceeds that of the brick or other structural or facing material, with the result that walls have a skeletal appearance even when the building is not of frame construction. When it is of frame

2

construction, the piers and spandrels may be in the same plane, or the spandrels may be recessed; in either case a fairly even balance is maintained between the vertical and horizontal lines (cf. Sullivanesque). A cornice of moderate projection is the commonest upper termination of the façade, though many have been removed in the interests of safety.

3

186   The Commercial Style

History: The first use of the term Commercial Style in print would seem to have been due to the anonymous editor of the four volumes of *Industrial Chicago*, published in 1891. "The Commercial Style," he wrote, "is the title suggested by the great office and mercantile buildings now found here. The requirements of commerce and the business principles of real estate owners called this style into life. Light, space, air and strength were demanded by such requirements and principles as the first objects and exterior ornamentation as the second." In this book we are limiting the term to the commercial architecture of the forty years 1875-1915 that is neither revivalist nor classifiable as Richardsonian Romanesque or Sullivanesque, as those terms are here employed.

In recent years it has been usual to regard Chicago as the birthplace of the Commercial Style as well as the city in which it reached its ultimate development. That its beginnings should be sought rather in New York and Philadelphia has been indicated by Winston Weisman, who has shown, for example, that the First Leiter Building of 1879 in Chicago, designed by William Le Baron Jenney with an internal iron skeleton and external masonry piers, was probably inspired by the Shillito Store of 1877 in Cincinnati, designed by James McLaughlin. However, without seeking to add fuel to a "Chicago or the East?" controversy that could become too like the "Rome or the Orient?" controversy that for so long bedeviled discussions of the origins of medieval architecture, one may safely state that the Commercial Style thrived in Chicago as nowhere else. "In no other American city has commercial architecture become so exclusively utilitarian as in Chicago," wrote Montgomery Schuyler in 1896, and nowhere else can it be so readily studied today. It was in Chicago, too, that the technical means that made possible the most complete fulfillment of "the requirements of commerce and the business principles of real estate owners" were first generally employed, with the result that the metal building frame became known as "Chicago construction."

Jenney was the pioneer of the metal-frame building in Chicago, his first being the Home Insurance Building, built in 1884-1885 and demolished in 1931; it was also the first building in which steel beams were used. (Cast iron for columns and wrought iron for beams and joists had been the most advanced practice up to this time, although steel had been used by the bridge engineers for some fifteen years.) Despite its

more advanced form of construction, the façades of the Home Insurance Building were no more open than those of the First Leiter Building. Jenney's Second Leiter Building (now Sears, Roebuck) of 1889-1891 shows that he too felt that need for classical discipline which had led to the Second Renaissance Revival and appears so unequivocally in Sullivan's contemporary Wainwright Building in St. Louis; the upper six stories, with the pilasterlike piers linking them vertically (those at the corners enlarged, as in the Wainwright), stand upon the two lowest like a Roman temple upon its podium. For the Manhattan Building, also of 1889-1891, Jenney designed a complex centralized composition whose axiality is not readily perceptible from any normal viewpoint. Incidentally, there is good evidence that the bay windows of this and many other Commercial Style buildings in Chicago were employed for the sake of the floor space they "stole" rather than for extra light and ventilation, as is sometimes said.

Some of the most notable Commercial Style buildings of the 1880's were due to Adler and Sullivan (whose Wainwright Building at St. Louis, showing a specifically Sullivanesque treatment for the skyscraper, was not designed until 1890). Among those still standing at the time of writing are the Troescher Building (now the Chicago Joint Board Building) of 1884 and the Wirt Dexter Building (624-630 South Wabash Avenue) of 1887. But the greatest masterpiece of the Commercial Style came from the office of Burnham and Root. This is the sixteen-story Monadnock Block, designed by John Wellborn Root in 1889. Although frame construction was by then well established and had been used by Root in other buildings, the Monadnock has masonry bearing walls; what makes it altogether exceptional among Commercial Style buildings, however, is that its design, with the subtle curvature of the base and cornice and the chamfer of the corners, represents a creative transmutation of an architecture of the distant past, the Egyptian. Later Commercial Style buildings by Burnham and Company, as the firm became after Root's death in 1893, include the Reliance Building of 1895 and the Fisher Building of 1896, both steel-framed, bay-windowed structures in which Gothic moldings and ornament are employed without any attempt to Gothicize the design as a whole.

In the 1890's, Holabird and Roche, whose first great work was the Tacoma Building of 1887-1889 (demolished in 1929), became the most

5

successful firm of architects specializing in commercial work in Chicago. In the Marquette Building of 1893, which still stands, they abandoned the bay window, which played so important a part in the Tacoma and other early buildings of the firm, in favor of very broad rectangular windows extending the full width of the structural bay, with the spandrels set back behind the front plane of the piers. They repeated the Marquette façade system, with variations, in a large number of buildings, some of which are as purely skeletal as any built in pre-Miesian Chicago. Meanwhile Sullivan, who in the Troescher Building had employed the same system, though with piers of solid masonry, a decade before the Marquette went up, gave the Meyer Building (1893) and the Carson, Pirie, Scott and Company Store (1899) façades in which piers and spandrels are in the same plane, and it is the long horizontals of the sill lines that are unbroken.

The Commercial Style preserved its vitality in Chicago into the second decade of the twentieth century. Two of the best of the later examples still to be seen there are the Hunter (now Liberty Mutual) Building at Madison and Whacker Drive, built in 1908 to the designs of Christian A. Eckstrom, with façades of the Holabird and Roche type, and the Dwight Building of 1910-1911 at 626-636 South Clark Street, by Schmidt, Garden and Martin, a concrete-framed warehouse with a façade modeled on Carson, Pirie, Scott.

Bibliography references: 1, 10, 18, 20, 41, 55, 68, 72, 84

1. The First Leiter Building, Chicago, Illinois. William Le Baron Jenney, architect, 1879. (HABS, Library of Congress. Photo: Cervin Robinson)
2. Ayer Building (later known as McClurg Building and Crown Building), Chicago, Illinois. Holabird and Roche, architects, 1900. (HABS, Library of Congress. Photo: Cervin Robinson)
3. Flour Exchange Building, Minneapolis, Minnesota. Long and Kees, architects, 1892-1909. (Minnesota Historical Society)
4. Fisher Building, Chicago, Illinois. Burnham and Company, architects, 1896. (HABS, Library of Congress. Photo: Harold Allen)
5. Manhattan Building, Chicago, Illinois. William Le Baron Jenney, architect, 1889-1891. (HABS, Library of Congress)

Sullivanesque

Sullivanesque buildings are simple, clear-cut forms terminated with flat roofs and boldly projecting cornices. Windows may be arched or linteled or both in the same building. In a multistory building they are organized into vertical bands, between piers that rise unbroken through the greater part of the elevation and are either stopped under a cornice or linked at the top by arches; the spandrels under the windows are recessed behind the plane of the face of the piers. Doorways are often arched, the Syrian arch being a favorite form. Relief ornament, of terra cotta or of plaster, may appear almost anywhere on the building, but most often on cornices, spandrels, and doorways. The character of this ornament, which combines naturalistic and stylized foliage with a variety of linear interlaces and other repeating motifs, is more readily grasped from the illustrations than from any verbal description.

1

History:
"When the rising cost of land in the later nineteenth-century city made commercial buildings of more than six stories desirable and the passenger elevator made them practicable, architects were at a loss how to give unity to elevations for which there were no historical precedents. It was Louis Henry Sullivan who solved the problem, demonstrating his solution for the first time in the Wainwright Building at St. Louis, designed in 1890."

Such an account of the matter might have been acceptable a few years ago. Today, thanks to Winston Weisman, we are aware that the essentials of Sullivan's solution appeared in certain buildings in Philadelphia erected between 1849 and 1860. And these buildings Sullivan, who spent some months in Frank Furness's office there in 1873, after his year at M.I.T. and before his first experience of Chicago and his two years in Paris at the Ecole des beaux-arts, certainly knew.

Now that there is no longer any compulsion to claim every great architect of the past hundred years as a pioneer of the International Style, we can permit ourselves to recognize that Sullivan was a classicist under the skin. Few buildings satisfy the classical demand that a work of art should be a finite object with a beginning, a middle, and an end as completely as Sullivan's skyscrapers of the 1890's. It has often been pointed out that the Wainwright Building may be likened to a classical column: the first two stories correspond to the base of the column, the next seven to its shaft, with the equivalent of fluting in the recessed planes of the windows and spandrels, and the top story, with the rich terra-cotta frieze and terminal slab, to the capital. Sullivan repeated this tripartite scheme, with major variations in detail, in the Schiller Building, Chicago (1891), the Union Trust Building, St. Louis (1892), the Guaranty Building, Buffalo (1894), the Bayard Building, New York (1897), and in unexecuted designs for buildings in St. Louis and Chicago.

Classical, too, in the Wainwright Building is the thickening of the corner piers. This contravenes the doctrine often attributed to Sullivan that form follows function, for in a steel-frame building such as this the corner piers in fact have less to support than the intermediate ones. The same criticism may be made of the treatment of the vertical elements that rise through the third to ninth stories as identical piers, although only half of them contain load-bearing steel. This deception – if that is

2

the word – is repeated in the Guaranty (now Prudential) Building. In the Bayard (now Condict) Building, however, the alternate verticals are treated frankly as mullions, and to leave the spectator in no doubt as to their not being part of the main structure, Sullivan brings them down only to the sills of the third-floor windows. Henry and Gustav Trost, in the splendid Mills Building at El Paso, give Sullivan's formula a new rhythm through the differentiation of piers and mullions – here two mullions between each two piers. When completed in 1910, this was the world's highest reinforced-concrete building. In its near-contemporary, the Colcord Building in Oklahoma City, William A. Wells presents the nine-story "shaft" in terms of flat wall punctuated by paired windows without impairing the soaring effect sought by Sullivan. Near the other end of the scale, in the Robert Gere Bank Building at Syracuse, Charles E. Colton exploits the decorative potential of the Sullivanesque – with some admixture of Richardsonian Romanesque in the lower part of the façade.

In his style of ornament Sullivan supplied a generation of American architects with a substitute for the Art Nouveau ornament that flourished in continental Europe in the 1890's and early 1900's. Although Sullivan's ornament has sometimes been regarded as a branch of the Art Nouveau, the differences are greater than the resemblances. There is much more Gothic in Sullivan's ornament, especially in the treatment of foliage and other vegetable forms, than there is in Art Nouveau, and much less – indeed, really nothing – of Japan. For an elementary knowledge of plant life Sullivan recommended to designers *Gray's School and Field Book of Botany.* A book that may have influenced him in a more important way was *The Grammar of Ornament,* by Owen Jones (1856), to which he was introduced by his young draftsman Frank Lloyd Wright in the late eighties; this it may have done both through the plates – those of Celtic interlaces in particular – and through the text, for Owen Jones's chapter on "Moresque Ornament" contains things that Sullivan might have written himself.

Questions of inspiration aside, Sullivan's ornament is distinguished from Art Nouveau by its symmetry, by the firmness of the underlying geometry – it has none of the visceral quality of so much Art Nouveau – and by the unambiguous manner in which naturalistic and abstract forms are contrasted rather than interfused. Of the numerous

5

7

architects who employed Sullivanesque ornament, the greatest was Frank Lloyd Wright (who abandoned it quite early in his career, however); the one who rang the changes on it most successfully over a long period was George Grant Elmslie, who worked for Sullivan from 1888 until 1909, being responsible for much that was nominally his master's during the latter part of that period, and continued to work in the style down to World War I, in partnership with William Gray Purcell.

Bibliography references: 1, 5, 10, 12, 18, 20, 41, 55, 84, 96, 98, 103, 119

1. Francis Apartments, Chicago, Illinois. Frank Lloyd Wright, architect, 1895. Detail of wall. (Photo: Author)
2. Guaranty (now Prudential) Building, Buffalo, New York. Adler and Sullivan, architects, 1895. (HABS, Library of Congress)
3. Robert Gere Bank Building, Syracuse, New York. Charles E. Colton, architect, 1894. (New York State Council on the Arts. Photo: Gilbert Ask)
4. Madlener House (now Graham Foundation for Advanced Studies in the Fine Arts), Chicago, Illinois. Richard E. Schmidt, architect, 1902. Detail of doorway. (Photo: Cervin Robinson)
5. Wainwright Building, St. Louis, Missouri, Adler and Sullivan, architects, 1890-1891. Detail of doorway. (Photo: Richard Nickel)
6. House on Third Street, Tucson, Arizona. Henry Trost, architect, circa 1905. (Photo: Author)
7. Mills Building, El Paso, Texas. Trost and Trost, architects, 1910. (El Paso Chamber of Commerce. Photo: Darst-Ireland)

The Prairie Style

Most Prairie houses are of two stories, a few of three. Often single-story wings reach out in more than one direction; these wings, which may open up into porches or carports at their extremities, frequently (and obviously) contain a single large room. Roofs are low and may be hipped or of double pitch, with eaves projection equaled only in the Western Stick Style. Emphasis is on the horizontal; dormers are never used, and even the chimneys are presented as oblong masses. Ribbon windows with wooden casements carry on the theme of horizontality, which may be yet further developed by dark wood stripping that continues the sill line around the house; some vertical stripping may represent the studs of the wall frame behind the plaster – even half-timbered effects are found – but the corners of the building are usually free of any such accentuation. Piers supporting the roofs of porches or verandas are of rectangular plan and massive appearance. Sometimes the end of the house is clasped, as it were, between similar but much larger piers. The

tops of all piers, as also of the parapets of porches and steps and balconies, are strongly defined by projecting caps or copings.

Plaster over wood frame is the type of construction in which the fullest range of Prairie house motifs is seen. But brick is used too, both as the principal material and in combination with wood-frame construction.

History: Frank Lloyd Wright was the master of the Prairie house, and anyone who sets out to describe it and the rationale of its design has to acknowledge that it has been done better than he could hope to do it by Wright himself. "We of the Middle West," wrote Wright, "are living on the prairie. The prairie has a beauty of its own and we should recognize and accentuate this natural beauty, its quiet level. Hence, gently sloping roofs, low proportions, quiet sky lines, suppressed heavy-set chimneys and sheltering overhangs, low terraces and out-reaching walls sequestering private gardens." An extraregional influence on the Prairie house – though Wright was reluctant to acknowledge this – was Japanese architecture.

2

The first Prairie houses, the Bradley and Hickox houses at Kankakee, Illinois, were designed by Wright in 1900; what is generally regarded as the first masterpiece among them, the Willits House at Highland Park, Illinois, was designed in the very next year, 1901. The Kankakee houses have gables, while the Willits House has hipped roofs; between them, they show all the features of the wood-and-plaster type that Wright was to vary and recombine with infinite resourcefulness during the next ten years. In 1902, for the Heurtley House at Oak Park, Illinois, he employed brick, and this was the material of the largest of his Prairie houses, the Martin House at Buffalo, New York (1904), as well as of what is often reckoned the greatest, namely the Robie House in Chicago (1908), and of the last of them all, the Allen House at Wichita, Kansas (1917). The Beachey House at Oak Park (1906) is exceptional among Wright's Prairie houses in its combination of brickwork and plaster.

Although some have had their champions among the critics, none of the many other architects who built Prairie houses in the first two decades of this century really rivaled Wright in the mode – which is not

3

to say that several of them did not build some fine houses. Among them were George Maher and Robert Spencer, both born in 1864 and thus three years older than Wright. Another, by six years Wright's junior, was Hugh Garden, who as early as 1901 exhibited at the Chicago Architectural Club – the gathering place of the Prairie School, as it came to be called – a design for a house in Highland Park that might almost be mistaken for Wright's work. Two others, who both worked in Wright's Studio at Oak Park for considerable periods of time, were William Drummond and Marion Mahony. The latter, who was the first woman graduate of the M.I.T. School of Architecture, was responsible for some of the best of the perspective renderings of Wright's buildings that it has become fashionable to publish as "drawings by Frank Lloyd Wright"; her own architectural oeuvre is not too well documented but appears to include at least three Prairie houses, two of which (the Mueller houses of 1912 at Decatur, Illinois) captured Wright's manner success-

fully enough for him to exhibit them as his own. Walter Burley Griffin, who in 1911 became Marion Mahony's husband, was a more considerable architect who also worked for Wright and who between 1902 and 1913, when his success in the competition for the plan of Canberra took him to Australia, designed several notable Prairie houses. Griffin's office was taken over after his departure by Barry Byrne, who had entered Wright's Studio at the age of eighteen in 1902 and left it in 1909 to join another former apprentice of Wright, Andrew Willatzen, in Seattle, where the Clark House in The Highlands stands as a Prairie house product of their brief partnership. After his return to Chicago, Byrne developed a personal version of the Prairie house, seen at its best in the Clarke House at Fairfield, Iowa (1915). Here Sullivan's influence, as well as Wright's, is perceptible – in the general proportions as much as in the semicircular window. In Prairie houses by other architects Sullivan's influence appears in the form of ornament. This is the case with some

5

6

of those by Henry Trost, who worked for a period in Sullivan's office and who took the Prairie house as far from its nominal habitat as El Paso and Tucson.

By no means all the buildings classifiable as Prairie houses were the work of architects who had direct links with Chicago. In many early twentieth-century suburbs there are builders' houses whose design can only have been suggested by illustrations in the *Inland Architect* or other magazines publishing the type.

Bibliography references: 1, 10, 20, 22, 31, 40, 48, 55, 77, 90, 92, 98, 100, 101, 113, 116

1. The Willits House, Highland Park, Illinois. Frank Lloyd Wright, architect, 1901. (Photo: Author)
2. Beachy House, Oak Park, Illinois. Frank Lloyd Wright, architect, 1906. (Photo: Author)

3. Thorncroft, River Forest, Illinois, William Drummond, architect, circa 1910. (Photo: Author)
4. Carter House, Evanston, Illinois. Walter Burley Griffin, architect, 1910. (HABS, Library of Congress. Photo: Richard Nickel)
5. Clarke House, Fairfield, Iowa. Barry Byrne, architect, 1915. (Photo: *Inland Architect*)
6. House on Third Street, Tucson, Arizona. Henry Trost, architect, circa 1905. (Photo: Author)

The Western Stick Style

Emphatic expression of wood-framed structure in conjunction with accentuation of the horizontal characterizes this style. Roofs are broad and of gentle pitch; the eaves are of great projection, often with the rafters and purlins projecting further still, and in many cases are supported by diagonal struts or by more or less elaborate brackets constructed of straight stickwork. Over a gable the eaves may be perforated, or carried out as an uncovered extension of the roof frame. Beams and other horizontal framing members – most noticeably in the porches and verandas that are practically universal features of houses in the style – commonly project up to a foot or more outside the posts supporting them; lintels similarly may extend visibly some way to either side of the window openings. In porches and verandas the larger framing members are sometimes frankly built up of standard scantlings in duplicate, the general effect being of construction with a limited number of standard elements. Shingles are the commonest wall covering in the earlier examples of the style, vertical boards with battens in the more recent. Departures from the rectilinear, in either plan or elevation, are rare. This does not, however, preclude a free adaptation of the plan to the site.

2

The Western Stick Style

History: The Western Stick Style first appeared in California in the later 1890's. It is as much a development from the Shingle Style, which had reached the Pacific Coast a decade earlier, as a continuation of the Stick Style of the High Victorian period. From the latter it differs in its horizontality and its freedom from Gothic forms. Sometimes an indebtedness to the Swiss chalet is evident; however, the chief overseas influence is that of Japan.

For all its structuralism, the Western Stick Style may sometimes be seen as an application of the principles of the Picturesque to the special conditions of the West. This is certainly true of the houses of the brothers Charles Sumner and Henry Mather Greene, who opened their practice in Pasadena in 1893. Then, and in the early years of this century when their masterpieces (such as the Blacker House of 1907 and the

Gamble House of 1908) were built, Pasadena was not the well-wooded place it is today, and an important part of the purpose of the deep eaves and numerous minor projections of rafters and beams was to provide visual relief through shadow in the bare and brilliant setting.

The Greene brothers generally employed quite substantial framing; others favored the lightest stickwork, which sometimes seems to border on fragility. This extreme lightness of membering is seen in some of the works of Bernard Maybeck, the leading master of the style in the San Francisco region – for example, in the Town and Gown Club at Berkeley.

For a quarter of a century following the rise of the Spanish Colonial Revival, the Western Stick Style suffered eclipse. Then in the 1940's, the works of its early masters were rediscovered. Maybeck and the Greene

4

brothers were hailed as pioneers of modern architecture – somewhat to their dismay, since they had no liking for most of what went under that name. At the same time the critics noticed that there were certain architects of a later generation practicing in California who did work that clearly belonged to the same tradition of structuralism in redwood; one of the best was Harwell Hamilton Harris, whose wife, Jean Murray Bangs, was the first architectural historian to investigate that tradition. The term "Bay Region Style" was promptly coined. Geographically it was hardly accurate, but there was much talk about the desirability of regionalism at the time and the term soon achieved international currency. What it stood for remained a potent force in the architecture of California and the Northwest to the end of the fifties, at least. There are many buildings in California by William Wilson Wurster, Joseph Esherick, and Charles Warren Callister and others in Oregon by John Yeon, for example, which, for all their differences from the work of Maybeck and the Greene brothers, represent the Western Stick Style in its latest, if not final, phase.

Bibliography references: 1, 9, 10, 13, 37, 78, 87, 107

1. Kelly House, Santa Barbara, California. Hudson Thomas, architect, 1915. (Photo: David Gebhard)
2. Blacker House, Pasadena, California. Greene and Greene, architects, 1906. (Photo: Author)
3. Hill House, Los Angeles, California. Albert R. Walker and John T. Vawter, architects, 1914. (Photo: Author)
4. Town and Gown Club, Berkeley, California. Bernard Maybeck, architect, 1899. (Photo: Author)

The Mission Style (1890 - 1920)

Arches and tiled roofs are the most general features of the Mission Style. The arches are usually semicircular, sometimes segmental – the two types may be combined in one building – and are quite free of moldings; the impost is marked by a stringcourse at most. The roofs are of low pitch and either hipped or stopped at the ends against shaped gables of curvilinear outline; sometimes they are entirely hidden by parapets. Walls are nearly always smooth-plastered. Balconies are frequent, and so, at least in larger buildings, are towers or turrets capped by domes or by pyramidal tiled roofs. There is a complete absence of sculptural ornament; this negative characteristic distinguishes Mission Style buildings from many, though by no means all, of those of the Spanish colonial Revival that followed.

History: The Mission Style is the Californian counterpart of the earlier Georgian Revival in the Eastern states. Like the latter, it was in some degree the result of disenchantment with the nineteenth-century present; it was also the result of a reaction against those Eastern styles which had

1

dominated the architectural scene in California since 1848, and which first came under attack in the Californian press in the early 1880's. On the positive side there was the boosterism of Charles Fletcher Lummis, the city editor of the *Los Angeles Daily Times* who became the best of the popular writers on the antiquities of California and the Southwest. The missions, wrote Lummis, "are worth more money, are a greater asset to Southern California, than our oil, our oranges, or even our climate."

Lummis was a New Englander by birth, and it was another New Englander, the architect Willis Polk, who in 1887 – the year after he arrived in San Francisco – made what would seem to have been the first Mission Style design to be published, a sketch for a "Mission Church of Southern California Type." Other architects, the Topeka-born Lester S. Moore of Los Angeles being among the first, took up the idea, but the Mission Style had to wait another six years for its first big public success in the California Building by A. Page Brown at the Columbian Exposition in Chicago. This was followed in 1894 by the same architect's Manufactures and Liberal Arts Building at the California Midwinter Fair in San Francisco. Brown was the most successful practitioner of the style in the

2

3

nineties; among the others working in it, beside Lester Moore, were J. P. Kremple, T. W. Parkes, and E. R. Swain. The Golden Gate Park Lodge of 1896 in San Francisco, designed by Swain, in which Mission arches and tiled roofs are combined with stonework of Richardsonian roughness, has been called "the best extant Mission Revival house in California." The largest Mission Revival building in California or anywhere else is certainly the Mission Inn at Riverside, built in 1890-1901 to the design of Arthur Benton; one of the largest outside California is another hotel, the Alvarado at Albuquerque, New Mexico (Charles F. Whittlesey, 1901-1905), which is among the earliest of a number of Mission Style hotels and stations built by the Santa Fe and Southern Pacific lines in the first decade of this century.

In 1904, a French journalist, Jules Huret, was quoted in *The Craftsman* as having written in *Figaro*,

The Mission Style

"Los Angeles is the first place in America where I have found original architecture. Not only does the style differ from any I have seen up to this time, but the buildings are of an adorable taste – ingenious and varied as Nature herself, graceful, elegant, appropriate and engaging. Many of the houses are in the style of the Spanish Renascence – 'Mission Style' – with almost flat roofs of red tiles, little round towers surmounted by Spanish-Moorish domes, and arcaded galleries, like the Franciscan cloisters of the past century. Others mingle the Colonial with the Mexican style, imitating the coarser construction of the adobe. All are very attractive and possessed of individuality."

It is unlikely that many of the houses praised by Huret would have more than period interest for us today. Nevertheless, two architects of real originality did work in the Mission Style. The older of them was Bernard Maybeck, whose Men's Faculty Club at the University of California, Berkeley, designed in 1900, is one of the few masterpieces in the style. The other was Irving Gill, who settled in San Diego in 1893, after two years in Chicago in the office of Adler and Sullivan. Gill himself wrote: "It is safe to say that more architectural crimes have been committed in their [the California missions'] name than in any other unless it be the Grecian temples." In such buildings as the Laughlin House at Los Angeles (1907) and the Women's Club (1913) and the Community Center (1914) at La Jolla, he used the vocabulary of the Mission Style while purifying its forms to produce an architecture of extraordinary clarity and directness.

Bibliography references: 7, 37, 63, 78, 97, 99

1. Union Pacific Railroad Station, Riverside, California. 1904. (Photo: Author)
2. House on Main Street, Tucson, Arizona. Henry Trost, architect, circa 1905. (Photo: Author)
3. Women's Club, La Jolla, California. Irving Gill, architect, 1913. (Photo: Author)

Bungaloid

The true bungalow is a small single-story house; the roof space may be made usable by a solitary dormer or by windows in the gables, but anything approaching a full second story disqualifies the building for the title of bungalow in the sense that was recognized by the builders and owners of this type of dwelling. The adjective Bungaloid is applicable also to the numerous houses that do their best to look like bungalows while having a second story – houses "built along bungalow lines," as they were called.

Bungalows came in many styles and partook of their respective characters so far as their small size, simplicity, and the usual need for economy permitted. If one had to choose a single building to represent the type, it would be of the Western Stick Style and would present two broad gables to the street, the gable of a porch-veranda in front being echoed by that of the body of the house behind and to one side.

1

Bungaloid

2

History: The word bungalow is a corruption of the Hindustani adjective *banglā,* which means "belonging to Bengal." By the end of the first quarter of the nineteenth century it was being used by the British in India to signify a low house surrounded by a veranda. Such houses were built by the Indian Government at intervals along the main roads to serve as resthouses for travelers, when they were called "dāk-bungalows." In India the bungalow was never thought of as anything more than a temporary or seasonal dwelling.

The first American house to be called a bungalow, according to Clay Lancaster, was one whose design was published in the *American Architect and Building News* in 1880. On the coast of Massachusetts, it was a two-and-a-half-story building and thus not really a bungalow in the sense of the term that was to become generally accepted. In California, where thanks to favorable climatic and social conditions the bungalow was to flourish as nowhere else (with the result that the term "California bungalow" became practically interchangeable with "bun-

3

galow" *tout court*), the first bungalow, so called, was built in 1895 on the San Francisco peninsula. Its architect was A. Page Brown, fresh from his Mission Style success at the Columbian Exposition; as Lancaster has observed, it suggested (at least in the *American Architect*'s illustration) an authentic Himalayan chalet.

There was nothing Indian except the name about the vast majority of later bungalows. Their designers most often drew from Japanese or Spanish sources – sometimes from both at once, as did the brothers Greene in the famous Bandini Bungalow at Pasadena (1903). This was planned around a patio in the Spanish manner but was of an extreme lightness of construction suggested by Japanese practice, the walls being of vertical redwood boards with battens over the joints. It had a numerous progeny of patio bungalows, as they were called, and the type of walling used in it, being very cheap, came into general use in California – though even there shingled walls, which the Greenes used in other bungalows, were probably always more common. The cobblestone

4

chimney was another feature that the Bandini Bungalow helped to popularize.

The bungalow had its heyday in 1900-1920, though tens of thousands of later houses are bungalows in nature if not in name. Sets of working drawings for bungalows could be bought for as little as five dollars, with the result that identical bungalows can be found in widely separated places; Los Angeles was the center of this trade. A book on bungalows, which went into three editions in the second decade of the century, divides American bungalows into nine types: the community bungalow of Southern California, the patio bungalow, the Swiss chalet type, the portable bungalow (including the tent house, which had walls of canvas stretched on hinged wooden frames), the retreat or summer house, the

Adirondack lodge (built of logs), the New England seacoast bungalow (Colonial in style), the Chicago (that is, Prairie Style) type, and "the house that is not a bungalow though built along bungalow lines." This is hardly a satisfactory classification, but one can only sympathize with the author in his difficulties. Certainly any attempt to classify bungalows by style categories would be beside the point, for in the minds of the designers of the best of them questions of style were secondary to considerations of planning – it was the bungalow as much as any other kind of house that led to the general adoption of the "living room" and the "outdoor-indoor" living space – of craftsmanship, climatic adaptation, and harmony with the landscape.

Bibliography references: 17, 37, 107

1. Bungalow, Coronado Street, Los Angeles, California. Circa 1910. (Photo: Author)
2. Bungaloid House, Coronado Street, Los Angeles, California. Circa 1910. (Photo: Author)
3. Bungalow, Gravilla Street, La Jolla, California. Circa 1910. (Photo: Author)
4. Crocker House, Pasadena, California. Greene and Greene, architects, 1909. (Photo: Author)

5: Styles That Reached Their Zenith in 1915-1945

The earliest styles of modernism (as that term was defined in the introduction to Part 4) were of limited application; office blocks and stores in one case and small-to-medium houses in the other two were the only types of building much affected by them. The Modernistic of the 1920's, being mainly a style of ornament, could be applied to all types, and to most of them it was. It also differed from the earlier modern styles in being of European inspiration. So was the International Style, in which ornament was abandoned altogether.

The Spanish Colonial Revival (1915 – 1940)

Red-tiled roofs of low pitch are as characteristic of the Spanish Colonial Revival as of the Mission Style that preceded it in the West; flat roofs may be surrounded by tiled parapets. Arches, though frequent, are not so nearly universal as they are in the Mission Style; houses, at least, may be entirely without them. Walls are plastered, a variety of textures being employed. There may be carved or cast ornament of considerable elaboration, usually concentrated around the openings. Doorways may be flanked by columns or pilasters. *Portales* may be of post-and-lintel type (often with bracket capitals, as in the Pueblo Style) or arcaded; in the latter case the arches may spring from either piers or columns. Balconies, with railings of wrought iron or of wood, are common features. So are window grilles, *rejas*, of wood with turned spindles or of iron. Windows often vary much in size in a single elevation, when they are asymmetrically disposed with broad expanses of wall between. The plans of houses, which are of two stories at most, take many forms. When there is a patio (which is not very often), it is rarely of the completely enclosed type. A favorite feature, belonging as much to the garden as to the house, is the pergola.

History: "Had they [the Franciscans in California] erected buildings similar to those of Mexico, the model, the inspiration, for our contemporary architects would have been wanting. The very elaborateness of these churches and monasteries would have precluded them from suggesting designs adapted to modern purposes." Thus did a writer discuss the Mission Style in *The Craftsman* in 1904. Eleven years later hundreds of thousands of visitors to the Panama-California Exposition at San Diego saw the most elaborate kind of Mexican Baroque adapted to the modern purpose of celebrating the opening of the Panama Canal.

The chief architect of the exhibition was Bertram Grosvenor Goodhue. In addition to being one of the leading Gothic Revivalists of the day, he was author of a book on Spanish Colonial architecture in Mexico, and it shows the way the wind was blowing that this should have been regarded as a most important qualification when he was appointed. The *pièce de résistance* among the individual structures was his California Building, an ecclesiastical-looking edifice whose façades and tower offer connoisseurs a test of their dexterity in disentangling Churrigueresque motifs from Morelia, Mexico City, Tepotzotlán, and San Luis Potosí.

The effect of the San Diego exhibition was such that although there were already in California some buildings (including a house by Goodhue) that might be classified as Spanish Colonial Revival rather than Mission, the beginning of that revival as a movement rather than a series of individual experiments may be dated 1915. In 1925, as Trent Sanford has said, Spanish architecture became a craze.

2

Today we are apt to find buildings of the Spanish Colonial Revival more palatable in inverse ratio to the amount of Plateresque or Churrigueresque ornament they display. Among those which can stand the application of less negative criteria are the works of the stockbroker-turned-painter-turned-architect George Washington Smith, who practiced in Southern California from 1916 until his death in 1930, and whose sure taste enabled him to maintain, in his best designs, a delicate balance between pictorial and more strictly architectural qualities. Other

3

Spanish Colonial revivalists of prominence in California were Carleton M. Winslow, who had been Goodhue's associate at San Diego, Edgar V. Ullrich, Richard Requa, Roy Sheldon Price, Wallace Neff, Frank Mead, Reginald D. Johnson, Myron Hunt, Elmer Grey, and the firm of Marston, Van Pelt and Maybury; in Florida there were Marion Syms Wyeth, Robert L. Weed, Addison Mizner, Kiehnel and Elliott, and Walter C. De Garmo.

The Spanish Colonial Revival had some real if modest successes in urban architecture. Examples are the company town of Tyrone, New

4

Mexico (designed by Goodhue in 1916, long abandoned and finally destroyed for open-pit mining in 1967), the centers of Ajo, Arizona (William M. Kenyon and Maurice F. Maine, architects, 1916), and Ojai, California (Mead and Requa, 1916), and the complex of shops and offices called El Paseo at Santa Barbara, California (James Osborne Craig, 1922).

Bibliography references: 5, 7, 14, 15, 26, 47, 69, 78, 99

1. Santa Barbara County Courthouse, Santa Barbara, California. William Mooser and Co., architects, 1929. (Photo: Author)
2. Neff House, San Marino, California. Wallace Neff, architect, 1929. (Photo: Author)
3. Brophy College Preparatory School, Phoenix, Arizona. John R. Kibbey, architect, 1928. (Photo: Author)
4. Sherwood House, La Jolla, California. George Washington Smith, architect, 1925-1928. (Photo: Author)

The Pueblo Style (1905 - 1940)

This is a massive-looking, archless style. Its special feature is the projecting roof beam, or *viga*, or at least a log professing to be such; the presence of vigas is alone enough to identify a building as Pueblo Style. In the more thoroughgoing examples they are accompanied by longer projections, the rainwater gutters, or *canales*. When not actually built of adobe, Pueblo Style buildings try to look as though they were. Some have battered walls; most have walls with blunt angles and irregularly rounded parapets; walls are always plastered when they are not of adobe, and usually when they are. Roofs are always flat; when the building is of more than one story, the stepped-up roofs of the Indian community house may be imitated. A veranda, or *portal,* with wooden posts that often have wooden bracket capitals, is a common feature.

History: Oddly enough, since the Indian and Spanish prototypes are confined to New Mexico and northern Arizona, where they constitute one of the few truly regional architectures in what is now the United

1

States, the Pueblo Style made its first appearance in California. Its initiator there was a Bostonian, A. C. Schweinfurth, with a hotel at Montalvo in 1894; in the next few years he followed this up with the Hearst Ranch at Pleasanton and a number of other buildings in the style.

In New Mexico the beginning would seem to have been the remodeling of a brick building on the campus of the University, at Albuquerque, in 1905. By 1911, this had been joined by a Pueblo Style central heating plant, dormitories (of adobe) for both sexes, and a fraternity house in the form of a kiva. W. George Tight, the president of the university, was the architect. His successor's preference for Mission led to a skirmish – not to dignify it by calling it a battle – of the styles, from which Pueblo emerged the victor, as is evident to any visitor to the campus today. Tight's championship of the Pueblo Style came from the same mating of archaeology and the booster spirit that had made Lummis the champion of the Mission Style in California. His aims, however, went beyond the revival of the visual characteristics of the regional architecture of New Mexico: the buildings of his university were eventually to coalesce into a gigantic academical pueblo. "The idea of the builders," we read, "was that no one of the buildings exists to itself, but that all will ultimately spread until they become parts of one enormous structure capable of accommodating all the population and giving room for all the varied activities of the University." In the late 1960's, this idea, never realized of course, seems remarkably modern.

In 1915, New Mexico was represented in the Panama-California Exposition at San Diego by a heavily "bevigaed" version of the church and convento at Acoma, designed by T. H. and W. M. Rapp, of Trinidad, Colorado. Less to be expected was the house at La Jolla, built four years later for Mrs. Wheeler Bailey, with Frank Mead and Richard Requa for architects, antiqued telegraph poles for vigas, and Hopi Indians for craftsmen and design consultants.

Back in New Mexico the brothers Rapp, in association with A. C. Henrickson, produced another version of the mission at Acoma for the Santa Fe Art Museum (1917). By the twenties the Pueblo Style was the thing for buildings of all sorts in New Mexico and had spread westward into Arizona. In hotel architecture – for which the Pueblo Style was first employed in New Mexico as early as 1909, in El Ortiz Hotel at Lamy (Louis Curtis, architect) – the Rapps and Henrickson achieved a popular

success with La Fonda, Santa Fe (1920). In the reinforced-concrete Hotel Franciscan at Albuquerque, completed in 1923, another partnership of brothers, Henry and Gustav Trost of El Paso, achieved another kind of success; they rose above historical eclecticism to design – as European critics recognized at the time – one of the very few American examples of the Expressionism of the half decade following World War I.

In the 1930's, several churches of seventeenth-century type were built on the Indian reservations in New Mexico to the design of Father Agnellus Lambert. This ecclesiastical phase of the style, distinguished from most of what had gone before by superior craftsmanship as well as greater archaeological accuracy, culminated in the church of Cristo Rey, Santa Fe (John Meem, 1939).

3

The Pueblo Style is by no means dead or even moribund, to judge from appearances. Not only is it the suburban house builder's vernacular in Albuquerque and Santa Fe, a modernized version of it is still employed for major buildings of public or quasi-public nature – for example, the new Albuquerque airport, opened in 1966.

Bibliography references: 5, 69, 97, 99

1. Hotel Franciscan, Albuquerque, New Mexico. Trost and Trost, architects, 1922-1923. (Photo: Author)
2. Zimmerman House, Albuquerque, New Mexico. W. Miles Brittelle, architect, 1929. (Photo: Author)
3. Administration Building, University of New Mexico, Albuquerque, New Mexico. John G. Meem, architect, 1936. (Photo: Author)
4. La Fonda Hotel, Santa Fe, New Mexico. Rapp, Rapp and Henrickson, architects, 1920. (Photo: Author)

4

Modernistic

Modernistic is first of all a style of ornament. This ornament is predominantly rectilinear, with geometrical curves playing a secondary role. The commonest motifs of all are fluting and reeding, often flanking doors or windows or forming horizontal bands above them. Chevrons or zigzags and various frets are much employed. Such ornament is normally in very low relief with a flat front plane. Another type, of greater saliency, consists of square or oblong blocks and other rectangular projections composed symmetrically around entrances or forming repeating patterns across the upper stories. In frame buildings the piers are normally devoid of ornament, except sometimes at the top, while the spandrels show one or other of the customary types or, at the very least, are faced with a different material, probably contrasting in color or texture with the cladding of the piers. Polychromatic effects are achieved by a variety of means, ranging from the use of faïence for surfacing walls to the application of gold leaf.

Verticality is stressed in most Modernistic buildings. In skyscrapers, setbacks are universal features as a result of the zoning regulations in force by the middle 1920's in all major American cities, the building as a whole often having somewhat the appearance of having been chopped out of a single tall block of material; this effect is increased by the treatment of the piers, which as a rule are neither stopped under a cornice nor crowned with pinnacles.

History: The Exposition des Arts Décoratifs, held in Paris in 1925, supplied the impetus for the rise of Modernistic architecture in the later twenties. In the case of America, it did this less by exhibiting any stylistic consistency in the buildings housing it than by diffusing a sentiment for modernity and the notion that it could be achieved by means of decoration. Architects who had conceived of their task as the adaptation of past styles to present requirements abandoned historical eclecticism (when their clients permitted) for what was soon being called the modern movement – a term that for some years to come meant different things to different people. How clean the break could be is seen in the New York buildings of the so successful and (in his day) much admired Ely Jacques Kahn. His Arsenal Building at Seventh Avenue and 35th Street, completed in 1925, has a colossal pilaster order, in a very "free" classic, embracing the first four stories, his contemporary 550 Seventh

2

Avenue an arcade with Byzantine colonnettes below the first setback. But 2 Park Avenue, completed two years later, is purely Modernistic.

The motifs that Modernistic ornament in Europe owed to a belated vulgarization of cubism are less conspicuous in the American version of the style, at least as represented by the work of Kahn and Raymond Hood (for example, the latter's apartment house of 1928 at 3 East 84th

4

Street, New York, and his Daily News Building, completed in 1930). The sources of American Modernistic, it is safe to say, were largely cisatlantic. They surely include George Elmslie's version of Sullivanesque ornament and the ornament (of Mayan inspiration) of the concrete-block buildings designed by Frank Lloyd Wright and his son Lloyd in the early twenties.

In commercial architecture the biggest single influence was that of the design that won the second prize in the Chicago Tribune competition of 1922 for the Finnish architect Eliel Saarinen (and led to his settling in America). This project, which was praised in print by Louis Sullivan, established unrelieved verticality as the ideal for high buildings, while the freedom of its Gothic detail, in Henry-Russell Hitchcock's words,

5

"stylized nearly to the point of absolute originality," prepared the way for detail that at least in theory was completely independent of historical precedent. Another, earlier design by Saarinen, the tower of his railroad station in Helsinki, was the prototype of those Modernistic towers (for example, that of Bullock's Wilshire Department Store in Los Angeles; John and Donald B. Parkinson, 1928) whose top stages look as if they might be telescoped into the main structure below.

Few American towns are without examples of Modernistic architecture. During the ascendancy of the International Style they seemed to represent what was worst in the immediate past. Today they are not so much disliked as simply disregarded. Tomorrow they will doubtless be found to have period charm. Some of them – though perhaps not very many – must have more than that.

Bibliography references: 3, 10, 16, 43, 44

1. Casino Building, New York. Ely Jacques Kahn, architect, 1931. (Photo: Sigurd Fischer)
2. Luhrs Tower, Phoenix, Arizona. Trost and Trost, architects, 1928. (Photo: Author)
3. Bullock's Wilshire Department Store, Los Angeles, California. John and Donald Parkinson, architects, 1928. (Bullock's Wilshire. Photo: Fred R. Dapprich)
4. Apartment House on 84th Street, New York. Raymond M. Hood, architect, 1928. (Photo: Gottscho-Schleisner)
5. New Fliedner Building, Portland, Oregon. Remodeled by Richard Sundeleaf, architect, 1930. (Photo: Author)

The International Style (1920-45)

The International Style is characterized by a complete absence of ornament and by forms in which effects of mass and weight are minimized for the sake of an effect of pure volume; compositionally, a balance of unlike parts is more often than not substituted for axial symmetry. Flat roofs, smooth and uniform wall surfaces, windows with minimal exterior reveals (which are perceived as continuations of the surface in another material rather than as holes in the wall), and windows that turn the corner of the building are among the means by which the effect of volume is obtained. Skeleton construction of steel or reinforced concrete is typical, though some smaller buildings are of wood with a sheathing of flush-jointed boards. Much use is made of the cantilever principle, both for carrying upper floors outside the supporting columns and for balconies and other projecting features. Wall surfaces of any material but wood are normally plastered and painted white; concrete

1

2

is almost never exposed. Horizontality – most marked in the ribbon window – and rectilinearity predominate, though circular windows, curved surfaces, and cylindrical forms sometimes appear as elements of contrast.

History: The International Style came into being in Europe in the 1920's. The countries in which it achieved its early successes were Germany, with Walter Gropius and Ludwig Mies van der Rohe as its leading practitioners, Holland, with J. J. P. Oud, and France, with Le Corbusier. It may

3

be said to have come of age in 1927. In that year all these and several other architects working in it were represented in the housing exhibition at Stuttgart known as the Weissenhofsiedlung, which was organized by Mies van der Rohe as First Vice President of the Deutsche Werkbund, a German government body that had as its purpose the improvement of industrial design. This was also the year in which Le Corbusier came close to winning the competition for the Palace of the League of

4

Nations, thus demonstrating the feasibility of the new architecture for major public buildings.

The International Style made its debut in the United States in 1928 when work began on the Lovell "Health" House at Los Angeles, designed by Richard Neutra for Dr. Philip Lovell, well known in the twenties for his books on health. Neutra had arrived in America from Vienna in 1923, going first to Chicago and then moving to California at the urging of his compatriot Rudolf Schindler. (In his earlier house for Dr. Lovell, at Newport Beach, Schindler emphasized structure to a degree that forbids its classification as International Style.)

In the East the first completed buildings in the new style were also houses – for example, those on Long Island by A. Lawrence Kocher and Albert Frey. But they were soon overshadowed by Raymond Hood's McGraw-Hill Building in New York, completed in 1931, and by the much finer Philadelphia Saving Fund Society building in Philadelphia, which went up in 1931-1932. The architects of P.S.F.S. were Howe and Lescaze. George Howe was a Philadelphian with a flourishing practice building houses in various historical styles for the Main-Liners when the P.S.F.S. commission came his way. It was due to him that the society accepted the International Style for its new headquarters, however much – and the question admits of dispute – its design may owe to his partner, William E. Lescaze. The latter was born and trained as an architect in Switzerland; his commitment to modernism was evidenced before the formation of the partnership in 1929 by a handful of buildings, interiors, and projects, designed during six years of independent practice in New York. Not only was P.S.F.S. the first skyscraper in which the principles of the International Style were consistently manifested; it is a building that has a place in any general view of the architecture of the twentieth century. Its importance was recognized at once by Henry-Russell Hitchcock and Philip Johnson, who included a photograph of it, still unfinished, in *The International Style: Architecture Since 1922.* (It was this book, published in 1932 in connection with the New York Museum of Modern Art's first exhibition of architecture, that defined the new style and gave it the name that, despite architects' qualms about the very word "style," has proved the most durable.)

In the 1930's, the growing acceptance of the International Style in many countries was counterbalanced by its proscription in Stalinist

Russia first and then in Nazi Germany. Nevertheless, it was the modern architecture of the decade, in the second half of which many architects who had worked in it in Europe settled in the United States. Among these were Mies van der Rohe, Gropius, and Marcel Breuer – leaders whose presence, it might be thought, would have had the effect of greatly reinforcing the International Style on this side of the Atlantic. However, Gropius and Breuer, after building houses for themselves at Lincoln, Massachusetts, which displayed the characteristics of the style in a quite doctrinaire manner, both deviated into other paths that may be supposed to represent concessions to American conditions – though as late as 1949 Gropius, working with a group of young architects called The Architects' Collaborative, or TAC, could still design the Harvard Graduate Center at Cambridge with scarcely a detail that he might not have used twenty years earlier. As for Mies, there had always been tendencies in his work, and even more in his philosophy of design, that were not fully consonant with International Style practice and principles, and in America he developed a style, personal and imitable at once, that is treated in the next section of this book under another heading.

The revolutionary style of the earlier twentieth century, by the late forties the International Style was under heavy fire from critics and architects alike. Today, as an independent entity, it is a thing of the past. But no architect of our time, whatever his opinion of the International Style, could design as if it had never been.

Bibliography references: 10, 11, 13, 104

1. Fitzpatrick House, Hollywood Hills, California. Rudolf Schindler, architect, 1936. (Photo: Julius Shulman)
2. Dunsmuir Apartments, Los Angeles, California. Gregory Ain, architect, 1937. (Photo: Julius Shulman)
3. Koosis House, Los Angeles, California. Raphael S. Soriano, architect, 1940. (Photo: Julius Shulman)
4. Graduate Center, Harvard University, Cambridge, Massachusetts. Walter Gropius and The Architects' Collaborative, architects, 1949-1950. (Photo: Robert Damora)

6: Styles That Have Flourished Since 1945

Only a small fraction of recent American architecture is represented by the styles illustrated here. If most of it seems unclassifiable, that may be because we are too close to it. Or it may be that a widespread desire for novelty, *plus* an eclecticism that in the professional journals has an unprecedented quantity of material to draw on, *minus* any generally accepted theory of architecture or agreement as to what constitutes architectural quality, is in truth productive of chaos.

1

Miesian

Rectangular forms of the utmost regularity and precision, a modular pattern established by the structural frame (which is most typically of steel, though fire regulations may cause it to be clad in concrete), glass walls, and over-all symmetry characterize Miesian architecture. In high buildings the ground-story walls are set back behind the outer piers; in some the grid of the frame is frankly expressed, while in others verticality is stressed with I-beams or "fins" rising uninterrupted through the upper stories. Outside stairs are broad and templelike; sometimes they are given a floating effect through the omission of the risers. A specifically Miesian type of roof consists of a slab hung from external beams supported at the ends only. Concrete and brick surfaces are exposed; when different materials are contiguous, their difference is emphasized by the detailing.

History: Ludwig Mies – van der Rohe was his mother's family name, which he adopted – was born at Aachen in 1886. When he migrated from Germany to the United States in 1938, he was one of the three acknowledged leaders in the International Style, with Le Corbusier and Gropius; at the same time he was the one with the fewest executed designs to his credit. Since then he has probably built as much as any other single architect living, while he has influenced a greater volume of building in America than any other architect in this century, even if Miesian architecture has never quite become "the American twentieth-century vernacular," as some prophesied that it would.

Mies's personal development of (and away from) the International Style began with the buildings of the Illinois Institute of Technology in Chicago, where he was appointed Director of Architecture soon after his arrival in America. The International Style architects, including Mies himself (even if he never carried the process as far as Le Corbusier did), exploited the freedom of plan and elevation that skeleton construction, by relieving walls of their structural duties, makes possible. In Mies's American work, on the other hand, the frame provides a discipline, comparable in some respects with that of the classical orders, within which expressiveness is achieved through the refinement of proportion and detail. Another basic difference is due to Mies's relatively low evaluation of use as a determinant of the plan. International Style buildings contain various spaces that are individualized, at least in theory, according to functional requirements; in Mies's buildings the larger spaces, at least, are of a generalized or "universal" nature that renders them adaptable to various functions.

First appearing as it did in Chicago, the city that half a century before had given its name to metal frame construction – "Chicago construction" it had been called in the 1890's – Mies's new style could be seen as constituting a revitalization (rather than a revival, with the unhappy connotations that term had in architectural circles) of an American tradition. It was peculiarly suited to, perhaps because it was in some degree inspired by, American technology. And by 1951, Mies had demonstrated its adaptability in buildings as different from each other, and from those on the I.I.T. campus, as the Farnsworth House at Plano, Illinois, and the twin apartment towers at 860 Lake Shore Drive, Chicago.

The two most famous of the earlier Miesian buildings by architects other than the master himself are the house of glass and steel at New Canaan, Connecticut, designed by Philip Johnson for his own use in 1949, and Lever House, New York, built in 1952 to the design of Gordon Bunshaft of Skidmore, Owings and Merrill. Both of them perhaps look rather less Miesian now than they did when they were new, though for different reasons. In the Johnson House the admitted debt to the Farnsworth House (designed three years before, though built a year

3

4

later) now seems less important than the anticipations of Johnson's later classicism. As for Lever House, it once looked Miesian enough despite the blue-green glass and the delicacy of the stainless steel grid of its curtain walls; but the weighty and symmetrical monumentality of a later work by Mies himself, the Seagram Building across Park Avenue a block to the south, tends to make one forget that the "floating" of the two rectilinear volumes in Lever House, the flat slab below and the tall one above, is an effect also seen in the Farnsworth House.

The protean Eero Saarinen was a Miesian when he designed the vast General Motors Technical Center at Warren, Michigan (1951-1956), in which he gave the style a festive air through the use of red, blue, and yellow glazed brick. His work soon took other directions, as did that of I. M. Pei after the Mile-High Center in Denver (1955). But Skidmore, Owings and Merrill's designers have continued to the present to explore the possibilities of the Miesian style in many of their numerous commissions; thus in Inland Steel, Chicago (1956-1958), they became the first to employ the "universal space" of Mies's single-story Farnsworth House and I.I.T. School of Architecture and Design for the floors of a multistory office building, while currently, in the Hancock Building designed by Bruce Graham, they are providing Chicago with a display of diagonal bracing such as it might have had earlier by building the Convention Hall that Mies designed in 1953. Another firm that has contributed handsomely to Miesian Chicago is C. F. Murphy Associates, most conspicuously with the twenty-three-story Continental Insurance Building (1962-1964) and the thirty-one-story, 630-foot Civic Center (1962-1965). The designer of both of these tower blocks, in the latter of which steel beams spanning no less than 87 feet are used, was Jacques Brownson, who had been a student under Mies at I.I.T. His steel-and-glass house of 1952 at Geneva, Illinois, is one of the most distinguished of the smaller Miesian buildings.

Bibliography references: 9, 10, 13, 24, 33, 84

1. Lake Shore Apartments, Chicago, Illinois. Ludwig Mies van der Rohe, architect, 1949-1951. (Photo: Rube Henry, Hedrich-Blessing)
2. Hull House Association Uptown Center, Chicago, Illinois. Crombie Taylor, architect, 1966. (Photo: Richard Nickel)
3. Hektoen Laboratory Building, Chicago, Illinois. C. F. Murphy Associates, architects, 1961. (Photo: Richard Nickel)
4. Brownson House, Geneva, Illinois. Jacques Brownson, architect, 1952. (Photo: Richard Nickel)

The New Formalism

The buildings of the New Formalism are typically self-contained, free-standing blocks, with strictly symmetrical elevations. Skylines are level, the building often being defined at the top by a heavy, projecting roof slab. Wall surfaces are always smooth and often glossy, a wide range of materials, natural and artificial, being used for facing. Columnar supports tend to be thicker and more fully modeled than in the International and Miesian styles, while the arch – altogether absent from both of them – appears in various shapes and may constitute the ruling motif of the design. Ornament is employed, most frequently in the form of patterned screens or grills of metal, cast stone, or concrete.

History: The ancient Roman architect Vitruvius wrote that the three essentials of architecture were *utilitas, firmitas,* and *venustas* – memorably rendered by Sir Henry Wotton in the seventeenth century as "commodity, firmness and delight." Most theories of architecture have laid special stress on one or another of the three. Thus in our time Miesian theory has emphasized firmness, that of the International Style, commodity. The architects of the New Formalism are unashamed in their pursuit of delight.

The means by which they seek to capture it are varied, ranging from the classicism of Philip Johnson to the ornamentalism of Minoru Yamasaki and the sentimental exoticism of Edward D. Stone (to name the three most prolific architects of the movement). All admire and imitate the past, showing a catholicity of taste that forbids one to classify the movement as a second Neo-Classical revival, as is tempting perhaps at first glance. All are agreed that the International Style is a thing of the past but not one to be imitated.

Johnson is the most interesting architect of the New Formalism. As early as 1949, his celebrated glass house at New Canaan, Connecticut, showed his classical inclinations in both its symmetry and the way in which it was firmly rooted in the earth instead of floating above it like Mies van der Rohe's Farnsworth House, which was the architect's admitted inspiration. In the Kneses Tifereth Israel Synagogue at Port Chester, New York, designed in 1956, the Miesian element is only residual, while there is much to remind the spectator of the Neo-Classicism of the late eighteenth and early nineteenth century – a vestibule of the oval form so much favored by Robert Adam and his followers, for example, and a hung ceiling that echoes the form of vaulting employed by the great English architect, Sir John Soane. In 1957, he paid tribute to an American Neo-Classical architect when he adopted the plan of Jefferson's University of Virginia for the University of St. Thomas, at Houston; here the individual buildings are strongly Miesian again. In the 1960's, a number of commissions for museums came his way. In two of them, the Amon Carter Museum of Western Art at Fort Worth (1961) and the Sheldon Memorial Art Gallery at the University of Nebraska (1963), he took the work of the Prussian Schinkel, architect of the Berlin Museum (1824-1828), as a point of departure. As for the miniature Museum for Pre-Columbian Art at Dumbarton Oaks (1963), where nine circular glass-walled rooms and no less than forty-eight columns of gargantuan stoutness are packed around a central court, all within a sixty-five-foot

square, it is tempting to see this as an elegant parody of that all-but-last monument of the twentieth-century Neo-Classical Revival, John Russell Pope's National Gallery – in which, in fact, the Pre-Columbian works of art at Dumbarton Oaks were first publicly displayed. In the façade of the New York State Theater at Lincoln Center (1962), Johnson went back to the seventeenth century, to the east façade of the Louvre in Paris, for the paired columns. (Since this motif was one of the chief items of the stock in trade of Beaux-Arts Classicism, its use by a former Miesian is not without a certain irony.)

The conscious allusiveness of Johnson's classicism makes him an architectural historian's architect; it does not make him an architect's architect. Stone and Yamasaki have been much more influential; their eclecticism is of a more generalized kind in that they set out to update past styles rather than develop the suggestions offered to the present by

3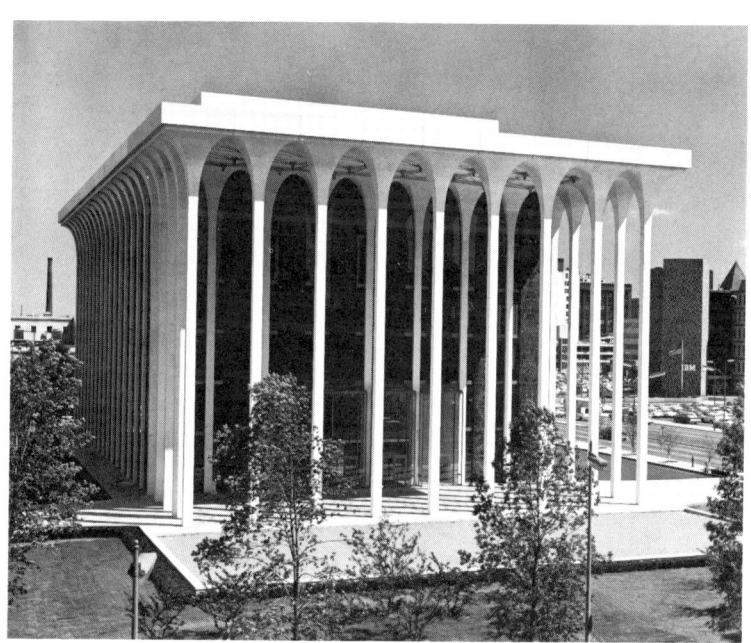

specific buildings of the past. Indeed, their influence has reached deep down through the lower layers of the architectural profession into the underworld of speculative building, for the acres of perforated cast-concrete screening that embellish the American subdivision are ultimately attributable to the example of Stone's New Delhi Embassy (1954-1958), while its metal equivalent (commoner in the commercial zones) would be seen less often than it is but for Yamasaki's moated Reynolds Metals office near Detroit (1959). And it is Stone, more than any other single architect, to whom we owe the return of the arch, though the inverted arcade, so popular with the designers of banks and real estate offices, has its source outside the United States in Oscar Niemeyer's presidential palace in the new capital of Brazil.

Although the buildings of the New Formalism are typically freestanding blocks with something of a temple air, their effect is sometimes Gothic rather than classical. This is the case with Yamasaki's College of Education at Wayne State University, Detroit (1960), although here to be sure it is of the Early Gothic Revival rather than of the Middle Ages themselves that one is so strongly reminded. A better, if rather labored, essay in Neo-Neo-Gothicism is Paul Rudolph's Mary Cooper Jewett Arts Center at Wellesley College (1958); here a desire to build in harmony with the Gothic Revival buildings on the campus was the motive for Gothicizing. Rudolph has done better in other manners. Skidmore, Owings and Merrill, however, have made some contributions to the New Formalism of a quality comparable to their best Miesian work – not perhaps in Bunshaft's ambiguously scaled Rare Book Library at Yale (1962) but certainly in the *palazzo*like Hancock Building in San Francisco (1959); here the return to functional dignity of the wall – for the external walls are bearing walls of reinforced concrete – is appropriately celebrated in a manner reminiscent, though not imitative, of Renaissance Italy.

The success of the New Formalism in the America of the 1960's is not hard to account for. In an affluent society it lends itself to the use of expensive materials (as well as of materials that only look expensive); in a society that aspires to culture it flatters the spectator with its references to the past; in a conservative society it suggests that old forms need only be restyled to fit them for new needs.

Bibliography references: 9, 32, 105

1. The Amon Carter Museum, Fort Worth, Texas. Philip Johnson, architect, 1961. (Amon Carter Museum. Photo: Glea Adams)
2. National Geographic Society, Washington, D.C. Edward Durell Stone, architect, 1962-1964. (National Geographic Society. Photo: Robert S. Oakes)
3. Northwestern National Life Insurance Company, Minneapolis, Minnesota. Minoru Yamasaki, architect, 1962. (Northwestern National Life Insurance Company. Photo: Balthazar Korab)
4. New Orleans Public Library, New Orleans, Louisiana. Curtis & Davis, Goldstein, Parham & Labouisse, Favrot, Reed, Mathes & Bergman, architects, 1958. (New Orleans Public Library)

Wrightian

Fundamentally homogeneous though superficially varied, Wrightian architecture is more easily recognized than described. A prevailing horizontality is one characteristic of nearly all of it; another is the importance given to the roof as a character-giving feature, whether it is a flat slab or of some pitched or "folded" form. In many designs the plan form is echoed in the elevations and also in any ornament there may be; a building with a plan based on the hexagonal figure will have diagonal glazing bars and a sloping roof ridge, for example, and a circular building a series of segmental arches. Battered walls are much employed; balcony

parapets are often inclined outward; piers frequently taper downward. Wood siding is most often horizontal, reinforcing the horizontality of the building as a whole; stone walling may imitate the natural stratification of the rock to the same effect. Concrete is either finished smooth or plastered and painted; in the Southwest and West "desert concrete," consisting of natural boulders held together by a great quantity of cement, is much employed. When two structural materials are used together, their textures are often strongly contrasted.

History: Frank Lloyd Wright's work between 1935 (when after a decade during which he built very little he entered upon what was virtually a second career) and his death in 1959 lends itself to classification under three heads, according to plan type: the rectangular mode, the

polygonal mode, and the circular mode. The rectangular mode is represented by the Usonian houses – Prairie houses brought up to date with flat roofs and certain structural and mechanical innovations – of the late thirties and the forties, by the incomparable Kaufman House, or Falling Water, at Bear Run, Pennsylvania (1935), and by various later houses; Wright's plans from the beginning had been predominantly rectangular, and this mode therefore does not mark any break with his own past. In the polygonal mode the plan is derived from other than quadrilateral figures, most frequently the hexagon. Wright's first design in this mode was made in 1928 for a health resort in Arizona, never built because of the Depression; his post-1935 buildings in it include the Hanna House at Palo Alto, California (1936), the chapel of Florida Southern College at Lakeland (1938), the Price Tower at Bartlesville, Oklahoma (1952), and

3

the Beth Sholom Synagogue at Elkins Park, Pennsylvania (1954). The first building of the circular mode, in which the plan is composed of circles and arcs, was the Johnson Wax Offices at Racine, Wisconsin, designed in 1936; others are the Guggenheim Museum in New York City (built in 1956-1959, though the first sketches were made in 1943), the Annunciation Greek Orthodox Church at Milwaukee (1956), and several houses, including the "Solar Hemicycle" house for Herbert Jacobs at Middleton, Wisconsin (1942), and one each for two of his sons, David and Robert Llewellyn Wright, at Phoenix, Arizona, and Silver Springs, Maryland (1950 and 1953).

Surprise that so strongly personal a style as Wright's should have so many imitators – for Wrightian buildings are scattered far and wide across the United States – is lessened when one realizes that many of them were trained by Wright himself in his Taliesin Fellowship, which was founded in 1932 and still continues as The Frank Lloyd Wright School of Architecture. Although the educational objective of the Fellowship was to imbue the "apprentice" with the principles of "organic architecture," in Wright's favorite phrase, and not to teach him how to imitate the more superficial aspects of the master's manner, the latter, as Wright recognized and sometimes lamented, was in many cases what it did. Of those who were trained in the Fellowship in the thirties and went on to develop their own personal versions of Wrightian architecture, Alden Dow in Michigan and John Lautner in Southern California are perhaps the best known, both having made their mark before Wright's death. After his death, the firm of Taliesin Associated Architects was formed, under the leadership of Wright's son-in-law, William Wesley Peters, in the first place to complete the jobs then in hand. With its headquarters at Taliesin West, the desert "camp" near Phoenix begun by Wright in 1938, and with its thirty-five associates licensed to practice in many states, this firm is responsible for a considerable volume of building, consistently Wrightian in character.

The most original of those architects who were not trained by Wright but have shown their admiration for him in executed designs is Bruce Goff. Born in 1904, Goff went through a Wrightian phase in his career – a phase in which his work was formally as well as conceptually related to Wright's – in the thirties and forties. In the fifties he had his office in Wright's Price Tower at Bartlesville. But by then he had moved on to a

5

kind of architectural *bricolage* – as the French call the employment of ready-made odds and ends for purposes for which they were not originally intended – that is unique.

Bibliography references: 9, 13, 49

1. Ascension Lutheran Church, Scottsdale, Arizona. Taliesin Associated Architects, architects, 1963. (Photo: Author)
2. Staley House, Madison, Ohio. Frank Lloyd Wright, architect, 1951. (Photo: Author)
3. Phoenix Art Museum, Phoenix, Arizona. Alden Dow, architect, 1958. (Photo: Author)
4. Gammage Memorial Auditorium, Arizona State University, Tempe, Arizona. Frank Lloyd Wright and Taliesin Associated Architects, architects, 1959-1963. (Photo: Author)
5. Library, Florida Southern College, Lakeland, Florida. Frank Lloyd Wright, architect, 1938. (Photo: Author)

Neo-Expressionism

In Neo-Expressionist buildings unity is achieved by continuity of form rather than proportional or geometrical means. Hence, sweeping curves, convex, concave, or faceted surfaces, and a tendency to avoid the rectangular wherever practicable; even structural columns and piers may "lean." When continuity is broken, the break is emphatic and even violent, with the result that acute angles and sharp-pointed gables are also characteristic. Arches and vaults of many forms are employed, but not the semicircular arch and barrel vault. The absence of these is due in part to the essentially static nature of the semicircle, which would conflict with the "movement" or "dynamism" of the style, and in part to their too obvious geometry, which would conflict with its generally sculptural effects.

History: As a movement in architecture, Expressionism had its beginnings in Germany around 1910 and flourished there and, with rather different results, in Holland for five or six years following the First World War. America was scarcely affected by it. Quite exceptionally, Barry Byrne, in search of a way on from the Prairie Style, was influenced by Hans Poelzig, one of the leading German Expressionists, in designing a couple of schools built in Chicago and at Wilmette, Illinois, in 1921-1923. Then there is the odd case of Trost and Trost's Hotel Franciscan at Albuquerque, mentioned and illustrated earlier in these pages under the heading of Pueblo Style, in which the form of some windows might be supposed to have been suggested by Rudolf Steiner's Goetheaneum at Dornach in Switzerland, did not chronology – the hotel was completed in 1923, the Goetheaneum begun in 1925 – rule out the possibility. If there were other examples of Expressionism in America in the twenties, as no doubt there were, they do not easily come to mind.

Neo-Expressionism became a force to be reckoned with in American architecture in the mid-fifties. The prefix is justified by the fact that the movement is not simply a continuation or resumption of the Expressionism of the teens and twenties. Nor is it, insofar as it is truly expressionist, a revival. The latter term normally implies the adoption of forms from past styles, and at the very center of the theory of Expressionism is the belief that forms are not to be adopted, or adapted; they should be the unique products of the marriage of the program – the architectural counterpart of the painter's subject – and the individual sensibility of the architect.

The popular view of Expressionism tends to stress the individual sensibility – the artist "expressing himself" – and forget or underrate the importance of the other partner to the marriage. This tendency has doubtless been encouraged by the recent success of that form of artistic parthenogenesis called Abstract Expressionism. In architecture there never has been, nor can be, such a thing as Abstract Expressionism. In architectural Expressionism – or Neo-Expressionism – the architect's first concern, at least in theory, is to express the essence of the program as he conceives of it. Thus Erich Mendelsohn, in the observatory at Potsdam built for Einstein in 1920, set out to express the nature of astrophysical research by suggesting the forms of optical instruments; thus Eero Saarinen, in the Trans World Airlines Terminal at Kennedy Airport, set out to express the idea of flight – not, despite the building's nickname, by imitating the form of a bird but with (in Allan Temko's words) "an abstraction of spatial liberty, expressed in continuous movement beneath the soaring roof." Sometimes it is the regional aspect of the program that the architect seeks to express. Herb Greene has related how before designing his house on the prairie near Norman, Oklahoma, he asked himself what the prairie meant to him and part of the answer was "birds" – accounting for that evocation of birds' wings by the layering of the shakes which is experienced even by those with no foreknowledge of the architect's intention.

At this point a distinction should be made between expressionism and symbolism in architecture. The roof of the First Unitarian Church at Madison, Wisconsin, which its architect Frank Lloyd Wright likened to a pair of praying hands, is an example of symbolism, as are the colonnades in front of St. Peter's, Rome, which their architect Bernini likened to the all-embracing arms of the church. An architectural symbol, once explained, may seem more or less apt; the point is that it has to be explained or understood by the spectator from his knowledge of the cultural context, and it does not in the long run greatly affect the spectator's aesthetic response to the work. In Expressionism, on the other hand, the architect tries to convey his message at a nonintellectual level and directly, through the very forms that he employs.

272 Neo-Expressionism

A more general consideration that forbids the classification of Wright as an Expressionist or a Neo-Expressionist is his method of working. Even those of his designs in the polygonal mode (as we have termed it) that might seem to earn him the title are developed from the plan, and by a strict application of geometry. The Expressionist, disdaining geometry or employing only those of its forms that have a "freehand" look, does not work this way; his way is nearer to the sculptor's. Saarinen, unchallenged as the leader of the movement during the last years of his life, was in fact trained as a sculptor. Other architects became Neo-Expressionists as a result of their admiration of what the engineers could do with matter, which is the sculptor's medium if the architect's is space. Had they not been assured by the great Spanish engineer Eduardo Torroja, speaking in Chicago, that the engineers could build anything that architects could design? The development of concrete shell vaults was a particular impetus, although the architects and the engineers have

2

3

not always seen eye to eye when it comes to shells – the architects, entranced by their elegance and lightness and the apparent freedoms that they confer, being apt to overlook their essential geometry, upon which the engineers insist. Another gift from the engineers was the catenary curve of the suspended steel-cable roof, first used on a monumental scale in Nowicki and Deitrick's Stock Judging Arena at Raleigh, North Carolina, in 1950, and later with full expressionist intent by Saarinen for the Ingalls Hockey Rink of Yale University (a structure whose dynamic effect was conveyed by a goalie in the words "Go, go, go!") and for Dulles Airport near Washington. The technique of spraying concrete ("gunite") over a metal armature – a technique by no means new to architecture, for the Greene brothers used it in California in 1913 – has lent itself to Neo-Expressionist effects in certain works by John Johansen, for example; in the Arizona desert near Scottsdale, Paolo Soleri has built by spraying mounds of earth on which the steel reinforcing rods have been laid, removing the earth by bulldozer and spade when the concrete has dried out.

A count of Neo-Expressionist buildings would probably show that churches and chapels constitute an absolute majority. One reason for this is that architects who normally work in other styles often turn Expressionist when commissioned to design a building for the practice of religion. Among those who have responded in this way are Harrison and Abramovitz, in the First Presbyterian Church at Stamford, Connecticut (1958), and Walter Netsch of Skidmore, Owings and Merrill, in the Air Force Academy Chapel at Colorado Springs (1960).

Bibliography references: 9, 45

1. Greene House, Norman, Oklahoma. Herb Greene, architect, 1960. (Photo: Julius Shulman)
2. Soleri Studio, Scottsdale, Arizona. Paolo Soleri, architect, 1961. (Photo: Author)
3. Dulles International Airport, Chantilly, Virginia. Eero Saarinen, architect, 1960. (Revere Copper and Brass)

Brutalism

Brutalist buildings have a look of weight and massiveness that immediately sets them apart from those of other predominantly rectangular, flat-roofed styles. Windows are treated as holes in the walls or as voids in the solids of the walls, and not (as in the International Style) as continuations of the "skin" of the building. Indeed, Brutalist buildings have no skin; this might be described as a "flesh-and-bones architecture." Concrete is the favorite material; it is always left exposed (as are brick and other materials – so far as fire regulations allow) and often rough-surfaced, showing the marks of the wooden formwork; sometimes it is textured by hammer or other means. Structure, most often concrete frame, is also frankly exhibited – as, inside the building, the plumbing and other services may be too. Broad, quiet wall surfaces are interrupted by deep-shadowed penetrations of the building mass; vertical slots may contrast with broad oblong openings or tall openings with horizontal slots, while "egg-crate" effects are also much employed.

History: If Reyner Banham, the historian of the movement, is to be believed, the term Brutalism is unique in the nomenclature of architecture

1

in that we owe it to the accident of an architect's nickname. The architect was the Englishman Peter Smithson, whose facial resemblance to the ancient Roman (as the busts represent him) led his friends in student days to call him Brutus. Not that the term Brutalism – or the New Brutalism, as it was at first – derived directly from that nickname, for it was coined by a Swedish architect, in Sweden, in 1950. In the following year it was brought to London, where it passed into colloquial currency among a group of like-minded architects that included Peter Smithson and his wife Alison. It soon occurred to someone that Peter Smithson's nickname gave the term a special sort of applicability to the Smithsons' work and philosophy; then Peter Smithson himself decided to take the application seriously and late in 1953 was responsible for the first appearance of the phrase "New Brutalism" in print. In 1954, what is always regarded as the first Brutalist building was completed. It was a public secondary school at Hunstanton, Norfolk; the architects, who had designed it in 1949, were Alison and Peter Smithson.

The Hunstanton school is a Miesian building of steel and brick; what makes it also a Brutalist one is the frank exposure of the electrical conduits, plumbing, and other services. That it can be Miesian and Brutalist at once is due to the fact that Brutalism, in its early phase, was not a style but a philosophy of design – as the Brutalists themselves had it, "an ethic, not an aesthetic." In this it was like High Victorian Gothic. (The Smithsons were admirers of William Butterfield, who as it happened laid out the town of Hunstanton where their school stands.) Nor were the ethics of the two movements, separated by exactly a century, at all dissimilar; both emphasized the special virtues of undisguised materials, for example, and both were opposed to Taste. An important difference appears, however, when we compare their respective attitudes to the recent past. The architects of the High Victorian Gothic could see nothing later than the Middle Ages of which they could honestly approve; the Brutalists, while despising the work of the generation that had started practice in the thirties, regarded themselves as the heirs to and guardians of the true principles of the twenties – of the principles of the International Style before it was so named and before it had, as they saw the matter, lost its sense of direction and purpose. That adherence to those principles did not imply the endless repetition of "white boxes"

was demonstrated not only by the example of Mies's American work but also by what Le Corbusier had been doing since the war – most conspicuously by the Unité d'Habitation at Marseilles, which with its internal street of shops is something more than a vast apartment block. In it Le Corbusier first employed *béton brut* – that is, concrete surfaces on which the marks of the rough wooden formwork are left exposed as an expression of the nature of the material.

Béton brut became so much a part of the image conjured up by the term Brutalism that until Banham set the record straight, first in the *Encyclopedia of Modern Architecture* and then in his monograph, *The New*

3

Brutalism, many must have thought that the term came from it. In America exposed concrete left in its rough state – or sometimes, as in Paul Rudolph's Art and Architecture Building at Yale (completed 1963), artificially roughened – is common to a great many, if not most, of the buildings to which the adjective Brutalist comes to be applied. Not all of these, perhaps, are Brutalist in the full sense of the term, and it is noticeable that Banham illustrates in his book only one American building of the last ten years, Paul Rudolph's Married Students' Housing at Yale (1962); in this (and in the house of Tasso Katselas, illustrated here) concrete and brick are combined in a manner that was first seen in Le Corbusier's two Jaoul houses of 1952 at Neuilly-sur-Seine. The influential Louis Kahn, whose Art Gallery at Yale (completed 1953) is often regarded as an example of proto-Brutalism, has shown more recently that neither his ethic nor his aesthetic is altogether that of Brutalism. And American architects have been less inclined to adopt "topological" planning than their English colleagues. Nevertheless, it is convenient to have a name for the style of mass, weight, roughness, and solidity that has become the most frequent medium of "advanced" architectural expression.

Bibliography references: 9, 13

1. Katselas House, Pittsburgh, Pennsylvania. Tasso Katselas, architect, 1962. (Photo: Marc Neuhof)
2. Wurster Hall (College of Environmental Design), University of California, Berkeley, California. Joseph Esherick, Donald Olsen, and Vernon De Mars, architects, 1960-1964. (Photo: Roy Flamm)
3. Christian Science Student Center, Urbana, Illinois. Paul Rudolph, architect, 1965. (Photo: Bill Engdahl, Hedrich-Blessing)

Bibliography

Only books published since 1915 are listed here as they are more likely to be available to the reader than earlier ones. Most of the standard works are listed; the other books and articles are those which were most helpful to the author and therefore may be helpful to the reader.

General Histories and Surveys, and Works of Criticism

1. Andrews, W., *Architecture, Ambition and Americans*. New York: Harper and Brothers, 1947.
2. Andrews, W., *Architecture in America: a Photographic History from the Colonial Period to the Present*. New York: Atheneum Publishers, 1960.
3. Cheney, S., *The New World Architecture*. New York: Longmans, Green and Company, 1930.
4. Early, J., *Romanticism and American Architecture*. New York: A. S. Barnes and Company, 1965.
5. Edgell, G. H., *The American Architecture of Today*. New York: Charles Scribner's Sons, 1928.
6. Gowans, A., *Images of American Living: Four Centuries of Architecture and Furniture as Cultural Expression*. Philadelphia and New York: J. B. Lippincott Company, 1964.
7. Hamlin, T. F., *The American Spirit in Architecture*. New Haven: Yale University Press, 1926.
8. Hamlin, T. F., *Greek Revival Architecture in America*. New York: Oxford University Press, 1944.
9. Heyer, P., *Architects on Architecture: New Directions in America*. New York: Walker and Company, 1966.
10. Hitchcock, H.-R., *Architecture: Nineteenth and Twentieth Centuries*. Baltimore: Penguin Books, 1958.
11. Hitchcock, H.-R., and Johnson, P., *The International Style*. New York: W. W. Norton and Company, 1966.
12. Kimball, S. F., *American Architecture*. Indianapolis: The Bobbs-Merrill Company, 1928.
13. McCallum, I.R.M., *Architecture U. S. A.* New York: Reinhold Publishing Corporation, 1959.

14. Newcomb, R., *Mediterranean Domestic Architecture in the United States.* Cleveland: J. H. Jansen, 1928.
15. Newcomb, R., *The Spanish House for America: Its Design, Furnishing, and Garden.* Philadelphia: J. B. Lippincott Company, 1927.
16. Onderdonk, F. S., *The Ferro-Concrete Style.* New York: Architectural Book Publishing Company, 1928.
17. Saylor, H. H., *Bungalows: Their Design, Construction and Furnishing.* New York: Robert M. McBride and Company, 1917.
18. Schuyler, M., *American Architecture and Other Writings.* Edited by William H. Jordy and Ralph Coe. Cambridge, Massachusetts: The Belknap Press of Harvard University Press, 1961.
19. Scully, V. J., Jr., *The Shingle Style: Architectural Theory and Design from Richardson to the Origins of Wright.* New Haven: Yale University Press, 1955.
20. Tallmadge, T. E., *The Story of Architecture in America.* New York: W. W. Norton and Company, 1927.

Biographies and Monographs

21. Baldwin, C. C., *Stanford White.* New York: Dodd, Mead and Company, 1931.
22. Birrell, J., *Walter Burley Griffin.* Brisbane: University of Queensland Press, 1964.
23. Cram, R. A., *My Life in Architecture.* Boston: Little, Brown, and Company, 1936.
24. Drexler, A., *Ludwig Mies van der Rohe.* New York: George Braziller, 1960.
25. Frary, I. T., *Thomas Jefferson, Architect and Builder.* Richmond: Garrett and Massie, 1950.
26. Gebhard, D., *George Washington Smith, 1876-1930: the Spanish Colonial Revival in California.* Santa Barbara: The Art Gallery, University of California, Santa Barbara, 1964.
27. Gilchrist, A. A., *William Strickland, Architect and Engineer.* Philadelphia: University of Pennsylvania Press, 1950.
28. Gray, D., *Thomas Hastings: Architect.* Boston: Houghton Mifflin Company, 1933.

29. Hamlin, T. F., *Benjamin Henry Latrobe*. New York: Oxford University Press, 1955.
30. Hitchcock, H.-R., *The Architecture of H. H. Richardson and His Times*. Revised edition. Cambridge, Massachusetts: The M.I.T. Press, 1966.
31. Hitchcock, H.-R., *In the Nature of Materials: the Buildings of Frank Lloyd Wright, 1887-1941*. New York: Duell, Sloan and Pearce, 1942.
32. Jacobus, J. M., Jr., *Philip Johnson*. New York: George Braziller, 1962.
33. Johnson, P., *Mies van der Rohe*. New York: Museum of Modern Art, 1947.
34. Kimball, S. F., *Mr. Samuel McIntire, Carver, Architect of Salem*. Portland, Maine: The Southworth-Anthoensen Press, 1940.
35. Johnson, P., *Thomas Jefferson, Architect*. Cambridge, Massachusetts: Riverside Press, 1916.
36. Lehmann, K., *Thomas Jefferson, American Humanist*. Chicago: University of Chicago Press, 1947.
37. McCoy, E., *Five California Architects*. New York: Reinhold Publishing Corporation, 1960.
38. McKim, Mead and White: *A Monograph of the Work of McKim, Mead and White*. 4 volumes. New York: The Architectural Book Publishing Company, 1915-1925.
39. Maginnis, C. D., *The Work of Cram and Ferguson, Architects*. New York: The Pencil Points Press, 1929.
40. Manson, G. C., *Frank Lloyd Wright to 1910*. New York: Reinhold Publishing Corporation, 1958.
41. Morrison, H. S., *Louis Sullivan, Prophet of Modern Architecture*. New York: Peter Smith, 1952.
42. Newton, R. H., *Town and Davis: Architects*. New York: Columbia University Press, 1942.
43. North, A. T., *Raymond M. Hood*. New York: McGraw-Hill Book Company, 1931.
44. Teegen, O. J., *Ely Jacques Kahn*. New York: McGraw-Hill Book Company, 1931.
45. Temko, A., *Eero Saarinen*. New York: George Braziller, 1962.
46. Upjohn, E. M., *Richard Upjohn, Architect and Churchman*. New York: Columbia University Press, 1939.
47. Whitaker, C. H., Editor, *Bertram Grosvenor Goodhue – Architect and*

Master of Many Arts. New York: Press of the American Institute of Architects, 1925.
48. Wright, F. L., *An Autobiography.* New York: Duell, Sloan and Pearce, 1943.
49. Wright, O. L., *Frank Lloyd Wright: His Life, His Work, His Words.* [With a list of the buildings and projects edited by B. B. Pfeiffer.] New York: Horizon Press, 1966.

Local and Regional Studies, Other Than Guidebooks

50. Alexander, D. B., *Texas Homes of the Nineteenth Century.* Austin: University of Texas Press, 1966.
51. Barnstone, H., *The Galveston That Was.* New York: The Macmillan Company, 1966.
52. Bunting, B., *Houses of Boston's Back Bay.* Cambridge, Massachusetts: The Belknap Press of the Harvard University Press, 1967.
53. Burnham, A., Editor, *New York Landmarks.* New York: Wesleyan University Press, 1964.
54. Cochran, G. A., *Grandeur in Tennessee: Classic Revival Architecture in a Pioneer State.* New York: J. J. Augustin, 1946.
55. Condit, C. W., *The Chicago School of Architecture.* Chicago: University of Chicago Press, 1964.
56. Dickson, H. E., *A Hundred Pennsylvania Buildings.* State College, Pennsylvania: Bald Eagle Press, 1954.
57. Downing, A., and Scully, V. J., *The Architectural Heritage of Newport, Rhode Island.* Cambridge: Harvard University Press, 1952.
58. Drury, J., *Historic Midwest Houses.* Minneapolis: University of Minnesota Press, 1947.
59. Frary, I. T., *Early Homes of Ohio.* Richmond: Garrett and Massie, 1936.
60. Hitchcock, H.-R., *Rhode Island Architecture.* Providence: Rhode Island Museum Press, 1939.
61. Hunter, W. H., Jr., Editor, *The Architecture of Baltimore: a Pictorial History.* Baltimore: The Johns Hopkins Press, 1953.
62. Kilham, W. H., *Boston after Bulfinch: an Account of its Architecture 1800-1900.* Cambridge: Harvard University Press, 1946.

63. Kirker, H., *California's Architectural Frontier: Style and Tradition in the Nineteenth Century.* San Marino: The Huntington Library, 1960.
64. Newcomb, R., *Architecture in Old Kentucky.* Urbana: University of Illinois Press, 1953.
65. Newcomb, R., *Architecture of the Old North-West Territory: A Study of Early Architecture in Ohio, Indiana, Illinois, Michigan, Wisconsin, and Part of Minnesota.* Chicago: University of Chicago Press, 1950.
66. Nichols, F. D., *The Early Architecture of Georgia.* Chapel Hill: University of North Carolina Press, 1957.
67. Peat, W. D., *Indiana Houses of the Nineteenth Century.* Indianapolis: Indiana Historical Society, 1962.
68. Randall, F. A., *History of the Development of Building Construction in Chicago.* Urbana: University of Illinois Press, 1949.
69. Sanford, T. E., *The Architecture of the Southwest.* New York: W. W. Norton and Company, 1950.
70. Steinbrueck, V., *Seattle Cityscape.* Seattle: University of Washington Press, 1962.
71. Syracuse University School of Architecture, *Architecture Worth Saving in Onondaga County.* New York: New York State Council on the Arts, 1964.
72. Tallmadge, T. E., *Architecture in Old Chicago.* Chicago: University of Chicago Press, 1941.
73. Tatum, G. B., *Penn's Great Town: 250 Years of Philadelphia Architecture Illustrated in Prints and Drawings.* Philadelphia: University of Pennsylvania Press, 1961.
74. Torbert, D. R., *A Century of Minnesota Architecture.* Minneapolis: The Minneapolis Society of Fine Arts, 1958.
75. White, T. B., Editor, *Philadelphia Architecture in the Nineteenth Century.* Philadelphia: University of Pennsylvania Press, 1953.

Guidebooks

Note: The State Guides originally compiled by the Federal Writers' Project of the W.P.A., a number of which have recently been reissued in revised editions by Hastings House, are often useful even though the sections on architecture contained in them vary greatly in quality and they are none too reliable when it comes to the attribution and dating of individual buildings.

76. American Institute of Architects Philadelphia Chapter, *Philadelphia Architecture.* New York: Reinhold Publishing Corporation, 1961.
77. Ballinger, B., *A Guide to the Architecture of Frank Lloyd Wright in Oak Park and River Forest, Illinois.* Oak Park, Illinois: Oak Park Public Library, 1966.
78. Gebhard, D., and Winter, R., *A Guide to Architecture in Southern California.* Los Angeles: Los Angeles County Museum of Art, 1965.
79. Hitchcock, H.-R., *A Guide to Boston Architecture, 1637–1954.* New York: Reinhold Publishing Corporation, 1954.
80. Huxtable, A. L., *Four Walking Tours of Modern Architecture in New York City.* Garden City, New York: Doubleday and Company, 1961.
81. Jacobsen, H. N., Editor, *A Guide to the Architecture of Washington, D.C.* New York: Frederick A. Praeger, 1965.
82. McClure, H. E., *Twin Cities Architecture: Minneapolis and St. Paul 1820-1955.* New York: Reinhold Publishing Corporation, 1955.
83. McCue, G., *The Building Art in St. Louis: Two Centuries.* St. Louis: The St. Louis Chapter, American Institute of Architects, 1964.
84. Siegel, A., Editor, *Chicago's Famous Buildings: a Photographic Guide to the City's Architectural Landmarks and Other Notable Buildings.* Chicago: University of Chicago Press, 1965.
85. Steinbrueck, V., *Seattle Architecture 1850-1953.* New York: Reinhold Publishing Corporation, 1953.
86. Wilson, S., Jr., *A Guide to Architecture of New Orleans 1699-1959.* New York: Reinhold Publishing Corporation, 1959.
87. Woodbridge, J. M. and S. B., *Buildings of the Bay Area: A Guide to the Architecture of the San Francisco Bay Region.* New York: Grove Press, 1960.

Articles in Periodicals

Note: This is a selection of articles of a historical nature published since 1945. For contemporary buildings the reader may consult the professional press, in particular *The Architectural Forum* and *The Architectural*

Record (both of which are indexed in the *Art Index*). The earlier issues of these magazines are a rich source of information about the architecture of the first half of this century. The *Avery Index to Architectural Periodicals* is an invaluable aid.

88. Andrews, W., "Alexander Jackson Davis," *Architectural Review* (London), CIX (May 1951), 307-312.
89. Baigell, M., "John Haviland in Philadelphia, 1818-1826," *Journal of the Society of Architectural Historians*, XXV, No. 3 (October 1966), 197-208.
90. Brooks, H. A., Jr., "The Early Work of the Prairie Architects," *Journal of the Society of Architectural Historians*, XIX, No. 1 (March 1960), 2-10.
91. Campbell, W., "Frank Furness, an American Pioneer," *Architectural Review*, CX (November 1951), 310-315.
92. Chappell, S. A., "Barry Byrne, Architect: His Formative Years," *Prairie School Review*, III, No. 4 (Fourth Quarter 1966), 5-23.
93. Creese, W., "Fowler and the Domestic Octagon," *Art Bulletin*, XXVIII (June 1946), 89-102.
94. Eckells, C. W., "The Egyptian Revival in America," *Archaeology*, III (September 1950), 164-169.
95. Forbes, J. D., "Shepley, Bulfinch, Richardson and Abbott, Architects: an Introduction," *Journal of the Society of Architectural Historians*, XVII, No. 3 (Fall 1958), 19-31.
96. Gebhard, D., "Louis Sullivan and George Grant Elmslie," *Journal of the Society of Architectural Historians*, XIX, No. 2 (May 1960), 62-68.
97. Gebhard, D., "Architecture and the Fred Harvey Houses," *New Mexico Architecture*, IV, Nos. 7 and 8 (July-August 1962), 11-17; VI, Nos. 1 and 2 (January-February 1964), 18-25.
98. Gebhard, D., "Purcell and Elmslie, Architects," with "A Guide to the Architecture of Purcell and Elmslie," *Prairie School Review*, II, No. 1 (First Quarter 1965), 5-24.
99. Gebhard, D., "The Spanish Colonial Revival in Southern California (1895-1930)," *Journal of the Society of Architectural Historians*, XXVI, No. 2 (May 1967), 131-147.
100. Greengard, B. C., "Hugh M. G. Garden," *Prairie School Review*, III, No. 1 (First Quarter 1966), 5-18.
101. Hasbrouck, W. R., "The Architectural Firm of Guenzel and

Drummond," *Prairie School Review*, I, No. 2 (Second Quarter 1964), 5-8.
102. Hersey, G. L., "Godey's Choice," *Journal of the Society of Architectural Historians*, XVIII, No. 3 (October 1959), 104-111.
103. Hope, H. R., "Louis Sullivan's Architectural Ornament," *Magazine of Art*, XL (March 1947), 111-117.
104. Jordy, W. H., "PSFS: Its Development and Its Significance in Modern Architecture," *Journal of the Society of Architectural Historians*, XXI, No. 2 (May 1962), 47-83.
105. Jordy, W. H., "The Formal Image: USA," *Architectural Review*, CXXVII (March 1960), 157-165.
106. Kramer, E. W., "Detlef Lienau, an Architect of the Brown Decades," *Journal of the Society of Architectural Historians*, XIV, No. 1 (March 1955), 18-25.
107. Lancaster, C., "The American Bungalow," *Art Bulletin*, XL (September 1958), 239-253.
108. Meeks, C. L. V., "Henry Austin and the Italian Villa," *Art Bulletin*, XXX (June 1948), 145-149.
109. Meeks, C. L. V., "Romanesque before Richardson in the United States," *Art Bulletin*, XXXV (March 1953), 17-33.
110. Omoto, S., "The Queen Anne Style and Architectural Criticism," *Journal of the Society of Architectural Historians*, XXIII, No. 1 (March 1964), 29-37.
111. Perusse, L. F., "The Gothic Revival in California, 1850-1890," *Journal of the Society of Architectural Historians*, XIV, No. 3 (October 1955), 15-22.
112. Pevsner, N., and Lang, S., "The Egyptian Revival," *Architectural Review*, CXIX (May 1956), 243-254.
113. Rudd, J. W., "George W. Maher, Architect of the Prairie School," *Prairie School Review*, I, No. 1 (First Quarter 1964), 5-10.
114. Scully, V. J., Jr., "Romantic Rationalism and the Expression of Structure in Wood: Downing, Wheeler, Gardner, and the 'Stick Style,' 1840-1876," *Art Bulletin*, XXXV (June 1953), 121-142.
115. Van Trump, J. D., "The Romanesque Revival in Pittsburgh," *Journal of the Society of Architectural Historians*, XVI, No. 3 (October 1957), 22-28.

116. Van Zanten, D. T., "The Early Work of Marion Mahony Griffin," *Prairie School Review,* III, No. 2 (Second Quarter 1966), 5-23.
117. Weisman, W., "Commercial Palaces of New York: 1845-1875," *Art Bulletin,* XXXVI (December 1954), 285-302.
118. Weisman, W., "New York and the Problem of the First Skyscraper," *Journal of the Society of Architectural Historians,* XII, No. 1 (March 1953), 13-21.
119. Weisman, W., "Philadelphia Functionalism and Sullivan," *Journal of the Society of Architectural Historians,* XX, No. 1 (March 1961), 3-19.
120. Wodehouse, L., "Ammi Burnham Young, 1798-1874," *Journal of the Society of Architectural Historians,* XXV, No. 4 (December 1966), 268-280.

Glossary

In most instances, the meanings given are limited to those carried by the terms in the text of this book. Some terms (for example, *spandrel*) have additional meanings that are not given here.
  Terms that have their own entries are printed in *italics*.

Acanthus A genus of thistlelike plants whose leaves were imitated in the ornament of the *Corinthian capital*.
Adobe Sun-dried brick (Spanish). In American usage the word also denotes a house built of the material.
Aisle In a church, the enclosed space on either side of the *nave*.
Anta A square pier finishing off the end of a wall in Greek temple architecture. Columns are said to be "in antis" when they stand within a porch between antae.
Anthemion A Greek architectural ornament in the form of a stylized representation of the flower of the honey-suckle.
Arcaded corbel table A row of *corbels* linked by arches.
Architrave The lowest part of an *entablature*. It is sometimes used by itself, for example, as an enframement around a window.
Astylar Without *columns* or *pilasters*.

Baroque architecture An architecture that originated in Rome at the beginning of the seventeenth century and spread from there over Europe and to the European colonies in the New World. *Classical* (Roman) forms are used, as in *Renaissance architecture*; generally speaking, Baroque architecture is more freely modeled than *Renaissance architecture* and exploits effects of light and shade in ways that the latter does not. There are many national and regional varieties of Baroque, some of which have their own names (such as *Churriguerresque*). It made way for *Neo-Classical architecture* in the second half of the eighteenth century.
Basilican Of a church, having an oblong *nave* flanked by lower *aisles*, with *clerestory* windows in the nave walls above the aisle roofs.
Battered Of walls, having faces that slope inward toward the top.
Belvedere A tower or turret built for the sake of the view.
Buttress A short section of wall built at right angles to one of the main outer walls of a building to help it resist lateral forces.

Canales Projecting gutters to throw the rain water off a roof and clear of the walls. (Spanish)
Cantilever A beam or bracket projecting from a wall or frame and stabilized by weight on its inner end.
Capital The uppermost part, or head, of a *column* or *pilaster*.
Casement A hinged window frame that opens horizontally like a door.
Caulicolus An ornament on the *capital* of the *Corinthian order* in the form of a curled fern shoot. (Latin for "little stalk.")
Chancel That part of a church which is reserved for the clergy and choir.
Chicago window An oblong window with a wide central *light* containing a fixed pane of plate glass flanked by narrower lights with *sashes*.
Churrigueresque A type of *Baroque,* characterized by very elaborate ornament, peculiar to Spain and Spanish America. Churriguerra was a Spanish architect who did not, as it happens, originate the style. But the term has been in use for a long time and is likely to continue in use until somebody offers an unexceptionable alternative.
Classical architecture The architecture of Ancient Greece and Ancient Rome, and architecture using forms derived from Ancient Greek and Ancient Roman architecture.
Clerestory The *nave* wall pierced with windows above the *aisle* roofs of a church.
Colossal order An *order* with *columns* or *pilasters* that run up through more than one story of the building.
Column A vertical support of round section. In classical architecture the column has three parts, base, shaft, and *capital;* the Greek *Doric* column is exceptional in that it has no base.
Composite order A classical *order* with *capitals* in which the *volutes* of the *Ionic* are combined with the *acanthus* foliage of the *Corinthian*.
Coping The top *course* of a wall.
Corbel A small projection built out from a wall to support the eaves of a roof or some other feature.
Corinthian order A classical *order* distinguished by the *capitals,* which are ornamented with *acanthus* leaves and *caulicoli*.
Cornice The uppermost, projecting part of an *entablature,* or a feature resembling it.
Coupled columns Columns that stand in pairs.

Course A horizontal row of stones or bricks in a wall.
Cupola A small domed structure rising from a roof or tower.
Curb A molded or otherwise ornamented edging along the top of the lower slopes of a *gambrel* or *mansard* roof.
Curtain wall An external wall for protection and privacy only, not forming part of the structure of the building.

Doric order A classical *order* most readily distinguished by its simple, unornamented *capitals* and the tablets with vertical grooving, called *triglyphs,* set at intervals in the *frieze.*
Dormer window An upright window lighting the space in a roof. When it is in the same plane as the wall, it is called a wall dormer, when it rises from the slope of the roof, a roof dormer.

Entablature The horizontal part of a classical *order,* above the *columns* or *pilasters.* It always has three parts, the lowest being called the *architrave,* the middle one the *frieze,* and the top one the *cornice;* the design varies in detail according to the *order* being used.

Fanlight A semicircular or semielliptical window above a door.
Flamboyant style The last style in French *Gothic architecture,* characterized by flamelike curves in *tracery* and *moldings.*
Flèche A small spire of wood and lead. (French: arrow.)
Fluting Vertical grooving, as on a Greek *column.*
Flying buttress A *buttress* of arched form, typically carrying lateral thrust from the wall of the *nave* across the *aisle* of a Gothic church.
Formwork A structure of wood (recently, sometimes of other materials) used to mold the surfaces of a concrete structure to the required shape and removed after the concrete has dried out.
Frame building A building in which the roof, walls, and floors are supported on a structural frame of wood, metal, or reinforced concrete.
Frieze The middle part of an *entablature.*

Gable The triangular upper part of a wall under the end of a ridged roof, or a wall rising above the end of a ridged roof.
Gablet A small *gable,* for example, over a dormer window.
Galerie The French name for a raised *veranda.*

Gambrel roof A roof with two slopes of different pitch on either side of the ridge.
Georgian Colonial architecture The architecture of the British colonies in North America from 1714 to 1776.
Gingerbread Pierced curvilinear ornament, executed with the jig saw or scroll saw, under the eaves of roofs. So called after the sugar frosting on German gingerbread houses.
Gorge and roll cornice A projection along the top of a wall consisting of a concave upper part and a thick *molding* or rounded section below, much employed in Egyptian architecture.
Gothic architecture The style of architecture, characterized by the use of the pointed arch, that arose in France a little before the middle of the twelfth century, spread to the rest of Western Europe during the next hundred years, and yielded to the Renaissance in Italy in the fifteenth century, elsewhere early in the sixteenth.
Greek fret A running ornament resembling a series of identical rectilinear labyrinths or mazes.

Half timbering A technique of wooden-frame construction in which the members are exposed on the outside of the wall.
Hipped roof A roof with slopes on all four sides. The hips are the lines of meeting of the slopes at the corners.

Impost The top of any vertical feature supporting an arch.
In antis See *anta*.
Ionic order A classical *order* distinguished by the form of the *capital*, with a spiral scroll, called a *volute*, on either side.

Jetty In framed buildings, an upper floor that projects a foot or two in front of the wall of the story below.

Lancet window A tall, narrow, pointed-arched window without *tracery*. A feature of *Gothic architecture*.
Light A section of a window.
Lintel A beam over an opening in a wall or over two or more *pillars* or posts.
Loggia The Italian for *veranda*.

Mansard roof A roof with two slopes to all four sides, the lower one being much steeper than the upper. It is named for the French seventeenth-century architect François Mansart.
Molding A projecting strip of curvilinear profile projecting from a surface of a building, or the curvilinear finishing of the edge of two meeting surfaces.
Mullion A vertical divider in a window.

Nave That part of a church in which the congregation (as distinct from the clergy) worships.
Neo-Classical architecture The architecture that followed *Baroque architecture* in the second half of the eighteenth century and prevailed until the middle of the nineteenth. It is distinguished from Baroque by its greater simplicity, its closer imitation of ancient classical models, and in many cases by the use of Greek forms.
Néo-Grec A French architectural style of the mid-nineteenth century, characterized by planar wall effects and simplified Greek and Roman detail, with *moldings* of flattened profile and incised linear ornament.

Order The basic structural system of the Greek temple, consisting of *columns* with an *entablature* resting on them. The Greeks had three orders, the *Doric,* the *Ionic,* and the *Corinthian;* the Romans adopted the Greek orders, adding them to their own *Tuscan;* the Renaissance adopted the Roman orders and added the *Composite.* Each order had its own recognized proportions as well as its own set of ornamental features.
Oriel window A bay window, especially one projecting from an upper story.

Palladianism A style of architecture modeled on the work of the North Italian architect Andrea Palladio (1518-1580). It was the dominant style in England from c. 1720 to c. 1760.
Palladian window A window with an arched central *light* and lower side lights with *entablatures* over them. It is also called a Venetian window.
Patera A small, flattish, circular or oval ornament employed in *classical architecture.*
Patio The courtyard of a Spanish house.

Pediment The *gable* end of the roof of a Greek or Roman temple, or a feature resembling it in *classical architecture*.
Pent roof An eaveslike feature projecting from a wall to throw off rain and snow.
Pergola A structure of posts or piers carrying beams and trelliswork for climbing plants.
Peripteral Having columns all around.
Perpendicular style The last style in English *Gothic architecture*, characterized by *tracery* in which the pattern is formed by multiplying the *mullions* in the upper part of the window and by a general tendency to stress vertical *moldings*.
Piazza The term used for a *veranda* generally in the colonial period, and in the South to this day. In Italy a *piazza* is an open space in a town, a square. When Inigo Jones planned the great square in Covent Garden, London, in 1631, he called it Covent Garden Piazza, to show off his Italian. To his fellow Londoners the arcaded walks (*loggie*, as Jones might have called them) surrounding the square seemed the most novel thing in the design. So they assumed that they were what the architect must have been referring to, and piazza got its new, Anglo-American meaning.
Picturesque, the A philosophy of landscape design and architecture according to which landscapes and buildings should exhibit qualities seen in, and should harmonize with each other as in, the pictures of the most admired landscape painters. It originated in England in the last quarter of the eighteenth century.
Pier (1) A stout *pillar* or *column*. (2) A vertical member in a metal or concrete building frame.
Pilaster A flat-faced representation of a *column*, in relief as it were, against a wall.
Pillar An upright support of rectangular horizontal section.
Pinnacle A vertical pointed feature, of stone or brick, employed to weight a *buttress* or a wall in *Gothic architecture*.
Pitch The degree of slope of a roof.
Plateresque A Spanish (and Mexican) type of *Renaissance architecture* characterized by ornament resembling silverwork (*platería*).
Portal In Spanish, a porch or *veranda*. Most often used in the plural, *portales*.

Portico A large porch having a roof, often with a *pediment,* supported by *columns* or *pillars.*
Purlin Part of a wooden roof frame, parallel with the ridge and connecting the *rafters.*

Quoin An outside corner of a building, or one of the stones or bricks forming an outside corner.

Rafter Part of a wooden roof frame, sloping down from the *ridge* to the eaves and establishing the *pitch.*
Reeding Vertical *moldings* resembling reed thatch, the convex counterpart of *fluting* as it were.
Reja A window grille or lattice. (Spanish).
Renaissance architecture A style of architecture characterized by the use of forms derived from Ancient Roman architecture that began in Florence around 1420, was taken up in other parts of Italy later in the fifteenth century, and in the rest of Western Europe in the sixteenth. The period 1420-1500 is called the Early Renaissance, 1500-1520 the High Renaissance, 1520-1600 the Late Renaissance or Mannerist Period. In many of the older histories of architecture (and some quite recent ones), all architecture from 1420 down to about 1750 is called "Renaissance." However, the accepted term for the architecture of 1600-1750 is now *Baroque.*
Ribbed vault A *vault* with arches (ribs) where the surfaces meet at an angle.
Ridge The horizontal line of meeting of the upper slopes of a roof.
Riser The vertical part of a step.
Rococo The last phase of *Baroque architecture,* characterized by double-curved forms and a shell-like type of ornament.
Romanesque architecture The style of architecture that prevailed in Western Europe from around A.D. 1000 until the coming of *Gothic architecture* – from c. 1140 to c. 1200, according to the region.
Rubble Stones that have not been shaped or at most have been shaped by fracture (not cut). In walls of coursed rubble the stones are of approximately the same size and shape and the courses are clearly defined; in random rubble the stones are of varying size and shape and the pattern formed by them is quite irregular.

Rustication Rough-surfaced stonework.

Sash A window frame that opens by sliding up or down.
Scantling (1) A piece of wood cut to a certain size. (2) The size to which a piece of wood is cut.
Shuttering Wooden boards between which concrete is poured in the construction of a concrete wall or pier and which are removed after the concrete has dried out.
Spandrel In a frame building, the wall immediately below an upper-story window.
Steeple The main vertical feature of a church, comprising both the tower and the spire or other superstructure.
Stringcourse A projecting *course* (sometimes two or three courses) forming a narrow horizontal strip across the wall of a building.
Syrian arch A type of semicircular arch that has very low supports, with the result that the distance from the *impost* to the level of the crown of the arch is greater than the height of the impost from the ground. It is so called because it was used in the Early Christian churches of Syria, in the fifth and sixth centuries.

Tabernacle frame An enframement for a doorway or window consisting of two *columns* or *pilasters* with an *entablature* and *pediment* above.
Trabeated Constructed with beams or *lintels*.
Tracery Ornamental openwork of stone in the upper part of a *Gothic* window. In Gothic Revival buildings it is sometimes of wood or of iron.
Transom A horizontal divider in a window.
Tuscan order A classical *order* most readily distinguishable by its simplicity. The columns are never *fluted,* the *capitals* are unornamented, and the *frieze* lacks the *triglyphs* that are part of the *Doric order.*

Vault A stone, brick, or concrete roof built on the arch principle, or an imitation of such in wood or plaster.
Venetian window See *Palladian window.*
Veranda A space alongside a house sheltered by a roof supported by posts, *pillars, columns* or arches. An earlier name for it in America was *piazza.* The French colonists called it a *galerie,* the Dutch a *stoep*

(Americanized as *stoop*), the Spanish a *portal;* in Italy it is a *loggia*. The term porch is best retained (as in this book) for a shelter over a door. Veranda comes from the Portuguese *varanda* and was first used by the British in India.
Viga Beam (Spanish).
Volute See *Ionic order*.
Voussoir A wedge-shaped stone or brick in an arch.

Zoning regulations Legal restrictions which were intended in the first place to relieve street congestion by regulating the height of buildings. The New York Zoning Act of 1916, the first American act of the kind and the model for most later ones, determined the permissible height of walls next to the street by two factors, the type of district or zone and the width of the street. Additional stories above this had to be set back behind a line drawn from the center of the street through a point at the top of the front plane of the street wall, except that upon one quarter of the total lot area the building could rise to any height.

Index

Aachen, Germany, 251
Abramovitz, Max (b. 1908), 274
Abstract Expressionism, 270
Academic Reaction, 167, 181
Acoma, New Mexico, San Estevan, 5, 230
Adam, Robert (1728-1792), 23, 26, 162, 258
Adam Style, vii, 21, 23-29, 34, 160
Adler, Dankmar (1844-1900), 188, 200, 216
Adler and Sullivan, 188, 200, 216
Ain, Gregory (b. 1908), 246
Ajo, Arizona, town center, 228
Albany, New York, cathedral project, 136
Albemarle County, Virginia, Estouteville, 33; Monticello, 32, 34
Alberti, Leone Battista (1404-1472), 157
Albuquerque, New Mexico, airport, 232; Alvarado Hotel, 215; Hotel Franciscan, 299, 232, 269; University of New Mexico, 230, administration building, 232; Zimmerman House, 231
Alden, Frank E. (d. 1908), 137
Aldrich, Chester H. (1871-1940), 163
Alexandria, Virginia, Lawrason Lafayette House, 28
American Architect and Building News, 218
American Builder, 117
The American Builder's Companion, by A. Benjamin, 41
The American Quarterly Review, 48
American Renaissance, 167
Anglo-Italian style, 180
The Antiquities of Athens, by J. Stuart and N. Revett, 23
Architects' Collaborative, The, 246
The Architecture of Country Houses, by A. J. Downing, 71
Arizona, health resort project (San Marcos in the Desert), 265
Arlington, Virginia, Lee Mansion, 45
Art Nouveau, 167, 195
Asheville, North Carolina, Biltmore, 145
Ashmont, Massachusetts, All Saints', 173
Athens, Georgia, Lyle-Hunnicutt House, 42
Athens, Greece, Monument of Lysicrates, 38, 42; Parthenon, 40, 164; Tower of the Winds, 38, 42
Atwood, Charles B. (1849-1895), 167
Augusta, Georgia, Ware-Sibley House, 25, 29

Austin, Henry (1804-1891), 49, 72
Austin, Texas, House House, 127

Bacon, Henry (1866-1924), 171
Badger, Daniel D. (1806-1884), 79
Baltimore, Maryland, Bryn Mawr College, 174; Calvert Street Station, 72, 73; Glen Ellen, 56; Homewood, 26; Homewood Villa, 72; Lovely Lane Methodist Church, 137; Sun Building, 79
Bangs, Jean Murray (Mrs. Harwell H. Harris), 212
Banham, P. Reyner, 275
Barnett, George I. (1815-1898), 108
Baroque style, vii
Barry, Sir Charles (1795-1860), 75, 179
Bartlesville, Oklahoma, Price Tower, 265, 267
Bay Region Style, viii, 212
Bear Run, Pennsylvania, Falling Water (Kaufman House), 265
Beaux-Arts Classicism, 149-153, 167, 169, 259
Belfast, Maine, Belfast National Bank, 92
Belle Helene, Geismar, Louisiana, 39
Belmead, Powhattan County, Virginia, 56
Beman, Solon S. (1853-1914), 145
Benes, W. Dominick (1858?-1935), 171
Benicia, California, State Capitol, 46
Benjamin, Asher (1773-1845), 29, 41
Benton, Arthur (1859-1927), 215
Berkeley, California, Town and Gown Club, 211; University of California, Men's Faculty Club, 216, Wurster Hall (College of Environmental Design), 277
Berlin, Germany, Altes Museum, 258
Bernini, Giovanni Lorenzo (1598-1680), 270
Betjeman, John, 179
Béton brut, 278
Binghampton, New York, Christ Church, 52
Bliesner (of Burnham and Bliesner), 153
Bloomfield Hills, Michigan, Cranbrook, 181
Bogardus, James (1800-1874), 79
Bonham, Texas, Brownlee House, 125
A Book of Architecture, by J. Gibbs, 11, 13
Books, influence on architecture of, 8
Borrominesque style, vii
Boston, Massachusetts, Arlington Street Church, 160; Cochrane House, 160; Commonwealth Avenue houses, 160; Customs House, 41; Foster-Hutchinson House, 8;

Boston, Massachusetts (*continued*)
Little House, 162, *163;* Old City Hall, *104,* 105; Old Museum of Fine Arts, 94; Old North Church, 13; Public Library, 130, 157; State House, 26; Trinity Church, 133-135
Bosworth, W. Welles (b. 1869), 171
Brasilia, Brazil, presidential palace, 260
Breuer, Marcel (b. 1902), 246
Bricolage, 268
Brigham, Charles (d. 1925), 94
Bristol, Rhode Island, Low House, 128
British Colonial architecture, 3-13
Brittelle, W. Miles (b. 1894), 233
Brooklyn, New York, Church of the Pilgrims, 63
Brown, A. Page (1859-1895), 214, 219
Brownson, Jacques (b. 1923), 255
Brutalism, 275-279
Bryant, Gridley J. F. (1816-1899), 105, 108
Bryant and Gilman, 105, 108
Bryn Mawr, Pennsylvania, Bryn Mawr College, 174
Buffalo, New York, Guaranty (Prudential) Building, 192, *193,* 195; Martin House, 203; Pan-American Exposition, Electric Tower, 152; New York State Building, 169
Buffington, Leroy S. (1848?-1931), 139
The Builder's Assistant, by J. Haviland, 46, 56
Building, 131
Bulfinch, Charles (1763-1844), 26, 162
Bungaloid, 147, 217-221
Bungalow, California, *218;* types of, 220-221
Bunshaft, Gordon (b. 1909), 252, 260
Bunting, Bainbridge, 142
Burlington, Charles City County, Virginia, *4*
Burlington, New Jersey, Doane House, 71; St. Mary's, *58,* 59
Burlington, Richard Boyle, third Earl of (1694-1753), 8
Burnham, Daniel H. (1846-1912), 137, 140, 188, 190
Burnham, Franklin P. (d. 1909), 153
Burnham and Bliesner, 153
Burnham and Company, 188, 190
Burnham and Root, 137, 140, 188
Butterfield, William (1814-1900), 89, 94, 276
Byrne, F. Barry (1884-1967), 205, 207, 269

California Architect and Building News, 124
California bungalow, 218
Callister, C. Warren (b. 1917), 212

Calvert, Texas, house, *121*
Cambridge Camden Society, 59
Cambridge, Massachusetts, Harvard University, Graduate Center, *244,* 246, Memorial Hall, 91; Massachusetts Institute of Technology, 171; Stoughton House, 128
Camden, Caroline County, Virginia, *68*
Camillus, New York, Baptist Church, *90*
Campbell, Colen (d. 1729), 8
Canberra, Australia, plan for, 205
Caroline County, Virginia, Camden, *68*
Carpenters' Gothic, 53
Carrère, John M. (1858-1911), 152
Carrère and Hastings, 152
Carroll, Charles, Jr., 26
Carter's Grove, James City County, Virginia, 8
Cary, George (1859-1945), 169
C. F. Murphy Associates, 255
Chambers, Sir William (1723-1796), 26
Chantilly, Virginia, Dulles International Airport, *273*
Character, 94, 96, 99, 111
Charles City County, Virginia, Burlington, *4;* Westover, 6, 8
Charleston, South Carolina, Brewton House, *7;* Drayton Hall, 8; Manigault House, 26; Russell House, 29; St. Michael's, *10,* 13
Charlottesville, Virginia, University of Virginia, *30,* 32, 258
Châteausque, 141-145
Chicago, Illinois, Auditorium, 139; Ayer (McClurg, Crown) Building, *184;* Ayer House, *135;* Borden House, *143;* Carson, Pirie, Scott and Company Store, 190; Civic Center, 255; Columbian Exposition, Administration Building, 152, California Building, 214, Fine Arts Building, 169; Continental Insurance Building, 255; Hektoen Laboratory Building, *253;* Home Insurance Building, 186; Hull House Association Uptown Center, *252;* Hunter (Liberty Mutual) Building, 190; Illinois Institute of Technology, 251, 252, 255; Immaculata High School, 269; Inland Steel Building, 255; Kimball House, *141;* Lake Shore Drive Apartments, *250,* 252; Lake View Presbyterian Church, 131; Lathrop House, 160, *164;* Leiter Building I, *183,* 186; Leiter Building II (Sears, Roebuck and Company), 188; Madlener House (Graham Foundation),

Chicago, Illinois (continued) 196; Manhattan Building, 188, 189; Marquette Building, 190; Marshall Field Wholesale Store, 137, 139; Meyer Building, 190; Monadnock Block, 188; Robie House, 203; Rookery, 138, 139, 140; St. Patrick's, 65; Schiller Building, 192; Tacoma Building, 188; Tribune Tower, 176; Troescher (Chicago Joint Board) Building, 188; University of Chicago, 175-176, Rockefeller Memorial Chapel, 176; Wirt Dexter Building, 188
Chicago Architectural Club, 204
Chicago construction, 186, 252
Chicago Convention Hall project, 255
Chicago Tribune Competition, 177, 239
Churrigueresque style, 225, 226
Cincinnati, Ohio, Shillito Store, 186; Taft House, 29
Clark, Henry Paston, 128
Clayton, Nicholas J. (1849-1916), 145
Cleaveland, Henry W., 111
Clérisseau, Charles-Louis (1722-1820), 23, 31
Cleveland, Ohio, Museum of Art, 166, 171; Old Stone Church, 64
Cobb, Henry I. (1859-1931), 139
Cockerell, Charles Robert (1788-1863), 100
Cole, Thomas (1801-1848), 46
Collegiate Gothic style, 174, 182
Colonial architecture, 3-19, British, 3-13, Dutch, 13, French, 14-16, Spanish, 5-8, 16-19
Colorado Springs, Colorado, Air Force Academy Chapel, 274
Colton, Charles E., 195, 200
Columbian Exposition, see Chicago, Columbian Exposition
Columbus, Ohio, State Capitol, 46
Commercial Style, 147, 183-190
Competitions, architectural, 133, 174, 239, 243
Concrete, 190, 238, 241, 272-273
Constructional coloration, 94, 99
Coolidge, Charles A. (1858-1936), 137, 140, 163, 165
Coolidge and Shattuck, 163, 165
Cope, Walter (1860-1902), 174, 181, 182
Cope and Stewardson, 174, 181, 182
Corbett, Harvey W. (1873-1954), 171
Cottage Residences, by A. J. Downing, 56, 71
The Craftsman, 215, 225
Craig, James O., 228

Cram, Ralph Adams (1863-1942), 173, 177
Cram, Goodhue and Ferguson, 173, 177
Cram and Wentworth, 173
Cronkhill, Shropshire, England, 71
Curlett, William (1845-1914), 140
Curlett, Cuthbertson and Eisen, 140
Curtis, Louis, 230
Curtis and Davis, 262
Cuthbertson, William J. (1850-1925), 140

Daniels, Howard, 47
Davis, Alexander Jackson (1803-1892), 41, 56, 60, 71
Day, Frank M. (1861-1918), 175
Day and Klauder, 175
Dayton, Ohio, Montgomery County Courthouse, 40
Decatur, Illinois, Mueller houses, 204
Decorated style, 53, 59
De Garmo, Walter C., 227
Deitrick, William H. (b. 1895), 273
Delano, William A. (1874-1960), 163
De Mars, Vernon (b. 1908), 279
Denon, Baron de, 48
Denver Colorado, Mile-High Center, 255
Detroit, Michigan, Public Library, 155, 158; Reynolds Metals Building, 260; Wayne University, College of Education, 260
Deutscher Werkbund, 243
Dinsmore, James, 35
Doane, George W., 71
Dornach, Switzerland, Goetheaneum, 269
Double-pile house, 8
Dow, Alden B. (b. 1904), 267, 268
Downing, Andrew Jackson (1815-1852), 41, 56, 71, 72, 111, 180
Doyle, Albert E. (1877-1928), 171
Drummond, William E. (1876-1946), 204, 206
Dubuque, Iowa, Langworthy House, 85
Dumbarton Oaks, see Georgetown, District of Columbia
Durham, North Carolina, Duke University, 175-176, chapel, 175
Dutch Colonial architecture, 13

Early English style, 53, 59
Early Gothic Revival, 53-60, 89, 94, 173, 174, 260
East Greenbush, New York, Bries House, 12
Eastlake, Charles Lock, 124

Eastlake, Sir Charles, 124
Eastlake Style, 123-126
The Ecclesiologist, 59
Eckstrom, Christian A., 190
Ecole des beaux-arts, Paris, 133, 150, 167, 192
Edwardian Baroque, 167
Egyptian Revival, 48-51
Eidlitz, Leopold (1823-1908), 67, 111
Elizabethan architecture, 179-180
Eisen Theodore (1852-1924), 140
Elkhorn, Wisconsin, octagon house, *83*
Elkins Park, Pennsylvania, Beth Sholom Synagogue, 267
Ellis, Harvey (1852-1904), 139
Elmslie, George G. (1871-1952), 199, 238
El Paso, Texas, Mills Building, 195, *199*; houses, 206
Emerson, William R. (1833-1918), 128
Encyclopedia of Modern Architecture, edited by W. Pehnt, 278
Esherick, Joseph (b. 1914), 212, 279
Estouteville, Albemarle County, Virginia, *33*
Evans, David, Jr., 26
Evanston, Illinois, Carter House, *204*; High School, 176
Exhibitions, buildings for, 152, 167, 169, 214, 225, 230, 235, 243
Expressionism, 232, 269

Fairfax County, Virginia, Mount Vernon, 25
Fairfield, Iowa, Clarke House, *205*
Farquharson, David, 82
Favrot, Reed, Mathes and Bergman, 262
Fellows, William K. (1870-1948), 177
Ferguson, Frank W. (1861-1926), 173, 177
Figaro, 215
Fisher, Elmer H., 140
Fishkill, New York, Fowler House, 86
Flamboyant style, 173, 174
Florence, Italy, Cathedral, 152; Pandolfini Palace, 75
Fonthill Abbey, Wiltshire, England, 53
Fortsville, Southampton County, Virginia, *35*
Fort Worth, Texas, Amon Carter Museum of Western Art, *256*, 258
Fouilhoux, J. André (1880-1945), 182
Fowler, Orson Squire, 85-86
Framing, metal, 184-185, *186*, 241; reinforced concrete, 190, 241

Francis I style, 142
Frankfort, Kentucky, State Capitol, 46
Frank Lloyd Wright School of Architecture, 267
Free Classic style, 118
Freeman, Frank (1861?-1949), 132
French Colonial architecture, 14-16
Frey, Albert (b. 1903), 245
Furness, Frank (1839-1912), 96, 192
Furniture, influence on architecture of, 123-124

Gallier, James, Jr. (1827-1868), 47
Galveston, Texas, Gresham House (The Bishop's Palace), *144*, 145
Gambier, Ohio, Kenyon College, 56
Garden, Hugh M. G. (1873-1961), 204
Gaynor, J. P., 79, 82
Geismar, Louisiana, Belle Helene, 39
General Grant style, 103
Geneva, Illinois, Brownson House, *254*, 255
Georgetown, District of Columbia, Customs House (Post Office), 76, *77*; Dumbarton Oaks Museum for Pre-Columbian Art, 258-259; houses, 72
Georgian Colonial architecture, ix, 32
Georgian Revival, ix, 159-165, 213
Germany, influence of, 14, 67, 269
Germantown, Pennsylvania, Cricket Club, 160, *162*; Mutual Fire Insurance Company Building, *116*, *117*; Pastorius House (Green Tree Inn), *15*
Gibbs, James (1682-1754), 11, 13, 160
Gilbert, Cass (1859-1934), 152, 158, 176
Gill, Irving J. (1870-1936), 216
Gilman, Arthur D. (1821-1882), 105, 108, 160
Goff, Bruce (b. 1904), 267-268
Goldstein, Parham and Labouisse, 262
Goodell, Nathaniel, 108
Goodhue, Bertram G. (1869-1924), 173, 174, 175, 228
Goodwin, Francis (1784-1835), 179, 181
Gori, Ottavian, 75
Gotch, J. Arthur, 181
Gothic, seventeenth-century survival of, 3
Gothic Revival, Early, 53-60, 89, 94, 173, 174, 260, High Victorian, 53, 89-96, 276, Late, 173-177
Gothic Rococo, 53
Graham, Bruce (b. 1925), 255
The Grammar of Ornament, by O. Jones, 195

Grand-Prix-de-Rome, 150, 169
Gray's School and Field Book of Botany, 195
Greene, Charles S. (1868-1957), *see* Greene and Greene
Greene, Henry M. (1870-1954), *see* Greene and Greene
Greene and Greene, 210, 212, 219, 221, 273
Greene, Herb (b. 1929), 270
Greene, John H. (1777-1850), 53
Greenwich, England, Queen's House, 158
Grey, Elmer, 227
Gries, John M. (1827-1862), 82
Griffin, Walter B. (1876-1937), 205, 207
Gropius, Walter (b. 1883), 243, 246, 251
Gunite (spray concrete), 273

Hackensack, New Jersey, Ackerman House, 13, *14*
Hadfield, George (circa 1764-1826), 45
Hale, Herbert D. (1866-1909), 171
Hale and Rogers, 171
Halicarnassus, Asia Minor, Mausoleum, 152, 171
Hamilton, John L., 177
Hamilton, William, 26
Hamlin, Talbot F., ix
Hampton-on-Thames, England, Garrick's villa, 26
Harding, George M., 96
Harris, Harwell H. (b. 1903), 212
Harrison, Wallace K. (b. 1895), 274
Harrison and Abramovitz, 274
Harrodsburg, Kentucky, Clay Hill, *22*
Hartford, Connecticut, Cheney Building, *134*
Hastings, Thomas (1860-1929), 152
Hatfield, R. G. (1815-1879), 79
Haviland, John (1792-1852), 46, 48, 56
Heard, Charles, 67
Helsinki, Finland, railroad station, 240
Henrickson, A. C., 230, 233
Highland Park, Illinois, design for house at, 204; Willits House, *201,* 203
High Victorian Gothic, 53, 89-96, 276
High Victorian Italianate, 97-101
Hingham, Massachusetts, Old Ship Meeting House, 5
Hints on Household Taste, by C. L. Eastlake, 124
Hints on Public Architecture, by R. D. Owen, 63

A History of the Gothic Revival, by C. L. Eastlake, 124
Hitchcock, Henry-Russell, 45, 63, 103, 115, 128, 135, 171, 179, 239, 245
Holabird, William (1854-1923), 188, 190
Holabird and Roche, 188, 190
Hollywood Hills, California, Fitzpatrick House, *241*
Home as Found, by J. F. Cooper, 46
A Home for All, by O. S. Fowler, 85
Home Place, St. Charles Parish, Louisiana, *16*
Hood, Raymond M. (1881-1934), 176-177, 238, 240, 245
Hood and Howells, 176-177
Hornbostel, Henry (1867?-1961), 152
Houston, Texas, University of St. Thomas, 258
Howard, John G. (1864-1931), 152
Howe, George (1886-1954), 245
Howells, John M. (1868?-1959), 177
Hubbell, Benjamin S. (1868?-1953), 171
Hubbell and Benes, 171
Huizar, Pedro, 19
Hunstanton, England, 276; Secondary School, 276
Hunt, Myron (1868?-1952), 227
Hunt, Richard Morris (1827-1895), 112, 133, 142, 145, 150, 152, 153, 158
Huret, Jules, 215, quoted, 216

Industrial Chicago, 186
Inland Architect, 206
Intentions in Architecture, by C. Norberg-Schulz, viii
International Style, 233, 241-246, 251, 257, 276
The International Style, by H.-R. Hitchcock and P. Johnson, 245
Ipswich, Massachusetts, Congregational Church, 55
Iron in building, 79, 154, 186
Italian Villa Style, 69-73
Ittner, William B. (1864-1936), 182

Jacobethan Revival, 178-182
Jacobs, Herbert, 265
James City County, Virginia, Carter's Grove 8
Japan, influence of, 195, 202, 210, 219
Jefferson, Thomas (1743-1826), 31-35, 38, 86, 258

Jeffersonian Classicism, 21, 31-35
Jenney, William Le B. (1832-1907), 186, 188, 190
Johansen, John M. (b. 1916), 273
Johnson, Philip C. (b. 1906), 245, 252, 257-259, 262
Johnson, Reginald D. (1882-1952), 227
Johnston, J. D., 132
Jones, Inigo (1573-1652), 11, 158
Jones, Owen, 195

Kahn, Albert (1869-1942), 182
Kahn, Ely J. (b. 1884), 235, 238, 240
Kahn, Louis I. (b. 1901), 279
Kankakee, Illinois, Bradley house, 203; Hickox House, 203
Katselas, Tasso G. (b. 1927), 279
Kees, Frederick (b. 1852), 140, 190
Kelham, George W. (1871-1936), 158
Kenyon, William M. (d. 1940), 228
Kibbey, John R., 228
Kiehnel, Richard (1870?-1944), 227
Kiehnel and Elliott, 227
Kirker, Harold, 140
Klauder, Charles Z. (1872-1938), 175, 176
Kocher, A. Lawrence (b. 1885), 245
Kremple, J. P., 215

Laconia, Indiana, Kintner-Winters House, 34
Lafever, Minard (1798-1854), 41, 49
La Jolla, California, Bailey House, 230; bungalow, *219*; Community Center, 216; Sherwood House, 228; Women's Club, *215*, 216
Lakeland, Florida, Florida Southern College, chapel, 265, library, *268*
Lamb, Hugo (1848-1903), 120, 130
Lamb and Rich, 120, 130
Lambert, Agnellus, 232
Lancaster, Clay, 218
Lancaster, Massachusetts, Christ Church, 26
Lancaster County, Virginia, Christ Church, *11*, 13
Langer, Suzanne, viii
Langley, Batty, 53
Lany, New Mexico, El Ortiz Hotel, 230
Late Gothic Revival, 173-177
Latrobe, B. Henry (1764-1820), 33, 38, 54
Lautner, John E. (b. 1911), 267
League of Nations competition, 243

Le Corbusier (1887-1965), 243, 251, 278, 279
Lefuel, H.-M. (1810-1880), 103
Lescaze, William E. (b. 1896), 245
Lewis, Ion (1858-1933), 158
Leyswood, Sussex, England, 115
Lexington, Kentucky, Loudoun, *54*
Lienau, Detlef (1818-1887), 142
Lincoln, Massachusetts, Gropius and Breuer houses, 246
Lincoln, Nebraska, University of Nebraska, Sheldon Memorial Library, 258
Little, Arthur (1852-1925), 128, 162, 165
Lombard style, 63, 67
London, England, All Saints, Margaret Street, 89, 94; Carlton Club, 79; Egyptian Hall, 48; Houses of Parliament, 179; Reform Club, 75; St. Martin-in-the-Fields, 13, 160, 163; Somerset House, 26; Travellers' Club, 75
London Foreign Office and War Office designs, 103
Long, Franklin B. (1842-1913), 140, 190
Long and Kees, 140, 190
Long Island, New York, houses, 245
Los Angeles, California, 220; Bullock's Wilshire Department Store, *237*, 240; bungaloid house, *218*; bungalow, *217*; County Courthouse, 140; Dunsmuir Apartments, 242; Grauman's Egyptian Theater, 50; Hill House, *210*; Koosis House, *243*; Langhlin House, 216; Los Angeles Heritage Society, *114*; Lovell "Health" House, 245
Los Angeles Daily Times, 214
Lovell, Philip, 245
Lowell, Guy (1870-1927), 171
Luce, Clarence S., 132
Lummis, Charles F., 214, 230
Lunenburg County Courthouse, Virginia, *32*
Lutyens, Sir Edwin (1869-1944), 163

McArthur, John, Jr. (1823-1890), 108
McClellanville, South Carolina, Hampton, 26
McIntire, Samuel (1757-1811), 26
McKim, Charles F. (1847-1909), see McKim, Mead and White
McKim, Mead and White, 120, 128, 137, 154, 157, 158, 160, 165, 169, 170, 171
McLaughlin, James W. (1834-1923), 186
McMurtry, John, 60
Madison, Ohio, Staley House, *264*

Madison, Wisconsin, First Unitarian Church, 270
Maher, George W. (1864-1926), 204
Mahony, Marion (Mrs. Walter B. Griffin), 204-205
Maine, Maurice F., 228
Manchester, England, Manchester Athenaeum, 75
Manigault, Gabriel (1758-1809), 26
Marlborough, Massachusetts, house, *45*
Marseilles, France, Unité d'Habitation, 278
Marston, Sylvanus B. (1863-1946), 227
Marston, Van Pelt and Maybury, 227
Masqueray, Emanuel L. (1861-1917), 152
Massachusetts Institute of Technology School of Architecture, 91, 192, 204
Matthews, Charles T. (1863-1934), 174
Mayan architecture, influence of, 238
Maybeck, Bernard R. (1862-1957), 152, 211, 212, 216
Maybury, E. W., 227
Mead, Frank, 227, 228, 230
Mead, William R. (1846-1928), 120, 128, 137, 154, 158, 160, 169, 170, 171
Meem, John G. (b. 1894), 232, 233
Memphis, Tennessee, Shelby County Courthouse, 171
Mendelsohn, Erich (1887-1953), 270
Merrill, John O. (b. 1896), 252, 255, 260, 274
Metuchen, New Jersey, St. Luke's, *113*
Meyer and Hollar, 50
Middleton, Wisconsin, Solar Hemicycle House, 267
Middletown, Rhode Island, Bookstaver House, *132;* Cram House, *110;* Joseph House, *131*
Mies van der Rohe, Ludwig (b. 1886), 243, 246, 251-252, 254, 255, 257, 278
Miesian, 251-255
Mills, Robert (1781-1855), 46
Milwaukee, Wisconsin, Annunciation Greek Orthodox Church, 267
Minneapolis, Minnesota, City Hall, 140; Flour Exchange Building, *185;* Hennepin County Courthouse, 139; Institute of Arts, *168,* 171; Northwestern Life Insurance Company Building, *259;* University of Minnesota, Pilsbury Hall, 139
Mission Style, ix, 178, 213-216, 225, 230
Mizner, Addison (1872-1933), 227
Modernistic, 223, 235-240

Montalvo, California, hotel, 230
Monticello, Albemarle County, Virginia, 32, 34
Mooser, William II (b. 1868), 228
Mount Airy, Richmond County, Virginia, 11
Mount Desert, Maine, house, 128
Mount Vernon, Fairfax County, Virginia, 25
Mullett, Alfred B. (1834-1890), 46, 106
Munich, Germany, Romanesque Revival in, 61
Murphy, Charles F. (b. 1890), 255
Museum of Modern Art, New York, 245

Napoleon III, Emperor of France, 103, 105
Nash, John (1752-1835), 63, 71
Nashville, Tennessee, First Presbyterian Church, 49
Neff, Wallace (b. 1895), 227, 228
Neo-Adamesque mode, 159-164
Neo-Classicism, vii, 19, 31, 257-258
Neo-Colonial mode, 159
Neo-Expressionism, 269-274
Neo-Grec style, 99
Neo-Neo-Gothicism, 260
Netsch, Walter A. (b. 1920), 274
Neuilly-sur-Seine, France, Jaoul houses, 279
Neutra, Richard J. (b. 1892), 245
Newark, New Jersey, County Courthouse, 48
New Bedford, Massachusetts, railroad station, 50; Rotch House, 59
New Brunswick, New Jersey, Jarrard House, 69; Smith House, *105*
New Brutalism, 276
The New Brutalism, by R. Banham, 278-279
Newburyport, Massachusetts, Dalton House, 9
New Canaan, Connecticut, Johnson House, 252, 257
New Delhi, India, United States Embassy, 260
New Formalism, vii, ix, 257-262
New Haven, Connecticut, Grove Street Cemetery, 49; Norton House, 72; Yale University, Art and Architecture Building, 279, Art Gallery, 279, Harkness Quadrangle and Memorial Tower, 175, Ingalls Hockey Rink, 273, Married Students' Housing, 279, Rare Book Library, 260
New Orleans, Louisiana, raised cottages, 15; Public Library, *261*
Newport, Rhode Island, The Breakers, *156,*

Newport, Rhode Island (*continued*) 157; Brick Market, 8; Crossways, 162; Edna Villa (Bell House), 128; Griswold House, *112;* King House, 72; Newton House, *159;* Ochre Court, 145; Sherman House, 115; Southside, 128; Taylor House, 160; Trinity Church, 13
Newport Beach, California, Lovell House, 245
Newport Parish, Virginia, Old Brick Church, *2,* 3
Newton, Dudley (1845?-1907), 112, 165
New York City, apartment house on East 84th Street, *238;* Arsenal Building, 235; Bayard (Condict) Building, 192, 195; Casino Building, *234;* Church of the Pilgrims, 63; Columbia University, 56; Continental Life Insurance Company Building, 105; County Courthouse, 171; Daily News Building, 238; Grace Church, 59; Grand Central Terminal, 152; Guggenheim Museum, 267; Halls of Justice (The Tombs), 48; Harper Brothers Building, 79; Haughwout Building, *78,* 79; Herald Building, 157; India House, *77;* Jefferson Market Courthouse (Jefferson Market Branch Library), *95;* Kennedy airport, Trans World Airlines Terminal, 270; Lever House, 252, 254-255; McGraw-Hill Building, 245; Metropolitan Museum of Art, *150;* National Academy, 94; New York State Theater, 259; New York University, 56; 2 Park Avenue, 238; Pennsylvania Station, *169;* Public library, 152; Racquet and Tennis Club, *157;* St. John the Divine, 174; St. Patrick's Cathedral, Lady Chapel, 174; St. Thomas's, 174; Seagram Building, 255; 550 Seventh Avenue, 235; A. T. Stewart Downtown Store, 75; Trinity Church, 59, 111; University Club, 157; C. Vanderbilt II House, 145; W. K. Vanderbilt House, 142; W. K. Vanderbilt, Jr., House, 145; Villard Houses, 154, 173; Woolworth Building, 176
Niernsée, John R. (1814-1885), 72
Niemeyer, Oscar (b. 1907), 260
Niles, Ohio, McKinley Memorial, 170
Nîmes, France, Maison Carrée, 31, 34
Nimmons, George C. (1865-1947), 177
Norberg-Schulz, Christian, viii
Norman, Oklahoma, Greene House, 270, *271*
Norman style, 63

Norwich, Connecticut, Converse House, *91;* Johnson House, *44*
Notman, John (1810-1865), 59, 63, 67, 71, 75, 77
Nowicki, Matthew (1910-1949), 273

Oak Park, Illinois, Beachey House, *202, 203;* Heurtley House, 203; Wright House, 131
Octagon Mode, 83-86
Ojai, California, town center, 228
Oklahoma City, Colcord Building, 195
Olsen, Donald (b. 1919), 279
Orders, the classical, 32, 33, 38, 41, 146, 251
Organic architecture, 267
Oud, J. J. P. (1890-1963), 243
Owen, Robert Dale, 63
Owings, Nathaniel A. (b. 1903), 252, 255, 260, 274
Oyster Bay, New York, Sagamore Hill, *118, 119*

Pain, William, 29
Palladian style, 8, 24
Palladio, Andrea (1518-1580), 32, 34
Palladio Londinensis, by W. Salmon, 8
Palmer and Hornbostel, 152
Palo Alto, California, Hanna House, 265; Stanford University, 137
Paris, France, Exposition des Arts Décoratifs, 235; Hôtel Cluny, 142; Louvre, 259; New Louvre, 103; Tuileries, 105
Parkes, T. W., 215
Parkinson, Donald B. (1895-1945), 240
Parkinson, John (1861-1935), 240
Pasadena, California, Bandini Bungalow, 219; Blacker House, *209,* 210; Crocker House, *220;* Gamble House, 211
Peabody, Robert S. (1845-1917), 128
Peabody and Stearns, 128
Pei, I. M. (b. 1917), 255
Pell, Francis L. (1873-1946), 171
Pell and Corbett, 171
Peripteral mode, 46
Perkins, Dwight H. (1867-1941), 177
Perkins, Fellows and Hamilton, 177
Permanent polychrome, 94
Perpendicular style, vii, 53, 59, 173, 174
Peruzzi, Baldassare (1481-1536), 158
Peters, W. Wesley (b. 1913), 267
Petersburg, Virginia, Battersea, *34*
Peterson, R. T., vii

Philadelphia, Pennsylvania, 192; Bank of Pennsylvania, 38, 41; Bartram Hall, 63; Centennial Exposition, British Government buildings, 117, state pavilions, 111; Christ Church, 13; City Hall, *102;* 108; Custom House (Second Bank of the United States), 40-41, 164; Eastern State Penitentiary, 56; Farmers' and Mechanics' Bank (Philadelphia Maritime Museum), *80;* George Gordon Building, *81;* Girard College, 45; Holy Trinity Church, *62,* 63; Independence Hall, 164; Masonic Hall, 55; Memorial Hall, *151;* Moyamensing County Prison, 48, *49;* Pennsylvania Academy of Fine Arts, *88,* 96; Pennsylvania Fire Insurance Company Building, 50; Pennsylvania Hospital, 26; Philadelphia Athenaeum, *74,* 75, 76; Philadelphia Bank, 55; Philadelphia Saving Fund Society Building, 245; St. Mark's, 59; Sedgeley, 54; University of Pennsylvania, *180,* 181; Woodlands, 25
Phoenix, Arizona, Brophy College Preparatory School, *227;* Luhrs Tower, *236;* Phoenix Art Museum, *265;* David Wright House, *267*
Picturesque Gothic, 53
Picturesque movement, 37, 54, 56, 61, 71, 76, 210
Piranesi, Giovanni Battista (1720-1778), 48
Pittsburgh, Pennsylvania, Allegheny County Buildings, 137; Allegheny County Soldiers and Sailors Memorial, 152; Calvary Episcopal Church, *172,* 174; Emmanuel Church, 136; First Baptist Church, 174; Katselas House, *275;* Shadyside Presbyterian Church, 137, *139;* University of Pittsburgh, Cathedral of Learning, 176
Plano, Illinois, Farnsworth House, 252, 255, 257
Plateresque style, 226
Platt, Charles A. (1861-1933), 163
Pleasanton, California, Hearst Ranch, 230
Poelzig, Hans (1869-1936), 269
Polk, Willis (1867-1924), 131, 214
Pope, John Russell (1874-1937), 152, 158, 171, 259
Port Chester, New York, Kneses Tifereth Israel Synagogue, 257
Porter, Lemuel (d. 1829), 29
Portland, Maine, Morse-Libby House, *70*
Portland, Oregon, Blagen Block, *97;* City Hall, *154;* Marks House, *100;* New Fliedner Building, *239;* United States National Bank, *170;* University Club, *178*
Post, Emily, 130
Post, George B. (1837-1913), 145
Potsdam, Germany, Einstein Observatory, 270
Potter, Edward T. (1831-1904), 91
Poughkeepsie, New York, store, 98; Vassar College, 105
Powhattan County, Virginia, Belmead, 56
Prairie Style, ix, 147, 210-206, 221, 265
Price, Bruce (1845-1903), 120, 130
Price, Roy Sheldon (1889-1940), 227
Princeton, New Jersey, Princeton University, 175, Graduate School, 175
Provençal Romanesque, 134
Providence, Rhode Island, St. John's Cathedral, 53; Union Station, 63
Pueblo Style, 225, 229-233
Pugin, Augustus W. N. (1812-1852), 59, 60
Purcell, William G. (1880-1965), 199

Queen Anne Style, 115-120, 142, 145

Racine, Wisconsin, Johnson Wax Administration Building, 267
Raised cottage, 15
Raleigh, North Carolina, State Capitol, 41; Stock Judging Arena, 273
Raphael, the painter (1483-1520), 75
Rapp, T. H. and W. M., 230, 233
Reality in architecture, 94, 96, 118
Reid, James M. (1851-1943), 132
Reid, Merritt J. (d. 1932), 132
Reidl, Joseph, 67
Renaissance Revival, North Italian Mode, 79-82, Romano-Tuscan Mode, 75-77, Second, 154-158, 160, 167, 173, 188
Renwick, James, 56
Renwick, James, Jr. (1818-1895), 56, 59, 63, 105
Requa, Richard S. (1880-1941), 227, 228, 230
Revett, Nicholas (1720-1804), 23
Rich, Charles A. (1855-1943), 120, 130
Richardson, Henry Hobson (1838-1886), 115, 128, 132, 133-137, 140, 150
Richardsonian Romanesque, ix, 133-140, 186, 195
Richmond County, Virginia, Mount Airy, 11

Richmond, Virginia, Medical College of Virginia, 49, *50;* State Capitol, 31
River Forest, Illinois, Thorncroft, *203*
Riverside, California, County Courthouse, *149;* Mission Inn, 215; railroad station, *213*
Rimini, Italy, S. Francesco, 157
Robinson, Peter F. (1776-1858), 48
Roche, Martin (1853-1927), 188, 190
Rogers, Isaiah, 46
Rogers, James Gamble (1867-1947), 171, 175
Romanesque Revival, 61-67
Romano-Tuscan Mode, *see* Renaissance Revival
Roman Revival, 35
Rome, Italy, Baths of Caracalla, 169; Cancelleria, 157; Colosseum, 79; English Coffee House, 48; Farnese Palace, 75; Massimi Palace, 158; Pantheon, 32; St. Peter's, 158; St. Peter's Piazza, colonnades, 270
Root, John W. (1850-1891), 131, 137, 188
Rouen, France, Palais de Justice, 142
Round Style, 63
Rudolph, Paul M. (b. 1918), 260, 279
Rural Homes, by G. Wheeler, 111
Ruskin, John, 91, 94
Russell, Archimedes (1840-1915), 96
Rutan, Charles H. (1851-1914), 137, 140

Saarinen, Eero (1910-1961), 255, 270, 272-273, 274
Saarinen, Eliel (1873-1950), 177, 239, 240
Sacramento, California, California State Bank, 140; Gallatin House (Governor's Mansion), *107*
Sag Harbor, New York, Whalers' Church, 49
St. Charles Parish, Louisiana, Home Place, *16*
St.-Gilles-de-Gard, France, abbey church, 137
St. Louis, Missouri, Bain House, *106;* Lionberger Warehouse, 137; Louisiana Purchase Exposition, Festival Hall and Cascades, 152; Old Post Office (Federal Building and Customs House), 106; Potter House, 128, *129, 130;* schools, 182; Union Trust Building, 192; Wainwright Building, 188, 192, *197*
St. Matthews, Kentucky, Ridgeway, 29
St. Paul, Minnesota, Church of the Assumption, *66;* State Capitol, 158
Salamanca, Spain, Old Cathedral, 134

Salem, Massachusetts, Adam Style buildings, 26
Salmon, William, 8
San Antonio, Texas, San José de Aguayo, *17,* 19
San Diego, California, Hotel del Coronado, 132; Panama-California Exposition, California Building, 225, New Mexico Building, 230
Sanford, Trent, 226
San Francisco, California, 124, 132, 211; Bank of California, 82; Buchanan Street, house on, *123;* California Midwinter Fair, Manufacturers and Liberal Arts Building, 214; double house on 21st Street, *122;* Golden Gate Park Lodge, 215; Hancock Building, 260; Mint, 46; Panama-Pacific International Exhibition, Palace of Fine Arts, 152, Tower of Jewels, 152; Public Library, 158; row houses, 124
San Luis Obispo, California, house, *109*
San Marino, California, Neff House, *226*
Sanmicheli, Michele (1484-1559), 82
Sansovinesque style, 79, 82
Sansovino, Iacopo (1486-1570), 79
Santa Barbara, California, County Courthouse, *224;* El Paseo, 228; Kelly House, *208;* mission church, 19
Santa Fe, New Mexico, Art Museum, 230; Church of Cristo Rey, 232; La Fonda, 232, *233*
Saugus, Massachusetts, Boardman House, *3*
Schenectady, New York, Union College, Nott Memorial Library, 89
Schindler, Rudolf M. (1887-1953), 245, 246
Schinkel, Karl Friedrich von (1781-1841), 171, 258
Schmidt, Richard E. (1866?-1959), 200
Schmidt, Garden and Martin, 200
Schuyler, Montgomery, 112, 120, 137, 139, 142, 186
Schwarzman, Herman J. (1843-1891), 153
Schweinfurth, Albert C. (1864-1900), 230
Scott, Sir Walter, 56
Scottsdale, Arizona, Ascension Lutheran Church, *263;* Soleri Studio, *272, 273;* Taliesin West, 267
Scully, Vincent, 111, 128
Sears, Roebuck and Company buildings, 177, 188
Seattle, Washington, Clark House, 205; Pioneer Building, *136,* 140

311

Second Empire Style, 103-108, 167
Second Renaissance Revival, 154-158, 160, 167, 173, 188
The Seven Lamps of Architecture, by J. Ruskin, 94
Shattuck, George C. (1864-1923), 163, 165
Shavian Memorial style, 115
Shaw, R. Norman (1831-1912), 115
Shell vaults, 272-273
Shepley, George F. (1860-1903), 137, 140
Shepley, Rutan and Coolidge, 137, 140
Shingle Style, 111, 118, 127-132, 145, 210
Short Hills, New Jersey, houses, 130
Shryock, Gideon (1802-1880), 46
Silsbee, James L. (1848-1913), 86, 131
Silver Springs, Maryland, Robert Llewellyn Wright House, 267
Skidmore, Louis (1897-1962), 252, 255, 260, 274
Skidmore, Owings, and Merrill, 252, 255, 260, 274
Sloan, Samuel (1815-1884), 63
Smirke, Sydney (1798-1877), 79
Smith, George Washington (1876-1930), 226, 228
Smithson, Alison M., 276
Smithson, Peter D. (b. 1923), 276
Snell, George (1820-1893), 160
Snell and Gergerson, 160
Soane, Sir John (1753-1837), 258
Soleri, Paolo (b. 1919), 273
Soriano, Raphael S. (b. 1904), 246
Southampton County, Virginia, Fortsville, 35
South Norwalk, Connecticut, Lockwood-Mathews Mansion, 142
Spalato, Dalmatia (Split, Yugoslavia), Diocletian's Palace, 23
Spanish Colonial architecture, in Arizona, 19, in California, 19, 225, in Mexico, 225, in New Mexico, 5, 8, 16, 229, in Texas, 19
Spanish Colonial Revival, 211, 213, 225-228
Spencer, Robert C. (1864-1953), 204
Springfield, Massachusetts, Municipal Buildings, 171
Stamford, Connecticut, First Presbyterian Church, 274
Starkweather, Nathan G., 72
Stearns, John G. (1843-1917), 128
Steel in building, 184-185, 186, 241
Steiner, Rudolf, 269

Stevens, John Calvin (1855-1940), 128
Stewardson, John (1859-1896), 174, 181, 182
Stewart, Thomas S., 49
Stick Style, 109-113, 167, 210, Western, 147, 201, 209-212, 127
Stone, Edward D. (b. 1902), 257, 259-260, 262
The Stones of Venice, by J. Ruskin, 94
Strickland, William (1788-1854), 42, 49, 55
Stuart, James (1713-1788), 23, 41
Sturgis, John H. (1834-1888), 94
Sturgis and Brigham, 94
Stuttgart, Germany, Weissenhofsiedlung, 243
Style, architects and the concept of, ix, nomenclature of, vii-viii, social purpose of, ix
Sullivan, Louis H. (1856-1924), 133, 188, 190, 192, 200, 205-206, 216, 239
Sullivanesque, 147, 186, 191-200, 238
Summerson, Sir John, 99, 100
Sundeleaf, Richard (b. 1900), 240
Swain, Edward R. (1852-1902), 215
Swansboro, North Carolina, Cedar Point, *84*
Symbolism in architecture, 270
Syracuse, New York, Robert Gere Bank Building, *194*, 195; Syracuse Savings Bank Building, *93*

TAC (The Architects' Collaborative), 246
Taliesin Associated Architects, 267, 268
Taliesin Fellowship, 267
Taliesin West, Scottsdale, Arizona, 267
Tallmadge, Ohio, Congregational Church, *27*, 29
Tarrytown, New York, Lyndhurst, 56
Taylor, C. Crombie (b. 1913), 255
Tefft, Thomas A. (1826-1859), 63
Temko, Allan, 270
Tempe, Arizona, Arizona State University, Gammage Memorial Auditorium, 266
Thomas, Griffith (1820-1879), 105
Thomas, Hudson, 212
Thornton, William (1759-1828), 26
Tight, W. George (1865-1910), 230
Torroja, Eduardo (1899-1961), 272
Town, Ithiel (1784-1844), 41
Town and Davis, 41
Townsend Harbor, Massachusetts, house, *51*
Transverse clerestory, 8

A Treatise on the Theory and Practice of Landscape Gardening, by A. J. Downing, 71
Trost, Gustavus A. (1876-1950), see Trost and Trost
Trost, Henry C. (1860-1933), 195, 200, 206, 207, 216, 232, 233, 240, 269
Trost and Trost, 195, 200, 232, 233, 240, 269
Trumbauer, Horace (1869-1933), 176, 177
Truth in architecture, 94, 96, 99, 111
Tucson, Arizona, house on Main Street, *216;* houses on Third Street, *198, 206;* San Xavier del Bac, *18,* 19
Tuxedo Park, New York, 130; Chandler House, 131
Tyrone, New Mexico, 227

Ullrich, Edgar V., 227
Upjohn Richard (1802-1878), 56, 60, 63, 72, 111
Urbana, Illinois, Christian Science Student Center, *278*
Usonian houses, 265
Utica, New York, City Hall, 72

Van Brunt, Henry (1832-1903), 91
Van Pelt, John V. (1874-1962), 227
Vanderbilt family, houses for, 142, 145
Vaux, Calvert (1824-1895), 72, 96
Vawter, John T. (d. 1958), 212
Venice, Italy, Doges' Palace, 94; St. Mark's Library, 79
Verona, Italy, Loggia del Consiglio, 157
Village and Farm Cottages, by H. W. Cleaveland, 111
Villas and Cottages, by C. Vaux, 72
Visconti, L.-T.-J. (1791-1853), 103
Vitruvius, Marcus, 257

Walker, Albert R., 212
Walter, Henry, 46
Walter, Thomas U. (1804-1887), 45, 48, 60
Ware, William R. (1832-1915), 91
Warren, Michigan, General Motors Technical Center, 255
Warren, Russell (1783-1860), 29, 50
Warren, Whitney (1864-1943), 152
Warren and Wetmore, 152
Washington, District of Columbia, All Souls Unitarian Church, *161,* 163; Brazilian Embassy, 158; Corcoran Gallery (Court of Claims), 105; Hitt House, 158; Lincoln Memorial, 171; National Gallery, 171, 259; National Geographic Society, *258;* Octagon (American Institute of Architects), 26; Smithsonian Institution, 63; State, War and Navy Department Building (Executive Office Building), 106; Temple of the Scottish Rite, 152, 171; United States Capitol, 26; United States Treasury, 46; Washington Club, 158
Washington, George, 25
Weed, Robert L. (1897-1961), 227
Weisman, Winston, 186, 192
Weissenhofsiedlung, Stuttgart, Germany, 243
Wellesley, Massachusetts, Wellesley College, Mary Cooper Jewett Arts Center, 260
Wells, Joseph Morrill (1853-1890), 154
Wells, William A., 195
Wentworth, Charles F. (1861-1897), 173
Western Stick Style, viii, 147, 201, 209-212, 217
Westover, Charles City County, Virginia, 6, 8
West Point, New York, United States Military Academy, 174
Wetmore, Charles D. (1866-1941), 152
Wheeler, Gervase, 111
Whidden, William H. (d. 1925), 158
Whidden and Lewis, 158
White, Stanford (1853-1906), 120, 128, 137, 154, 157, 158, 160, 165, 169, 170, 171
Whitehouse, Morris H. (1867-1944), 182
Whittlesey, Charles F. (1867-1941), 215
Wichita, Kansas, Allen House, 203
Wight, Peter B. (1838-1925), 94
Willatzen, Andrew, 205
Williams, Warren H., 101
Wills, Frank (d. 1856), 96
Wilmette, Illinois, St. Francis Xavier High School, 269
Wilmington, North Carolina, St. James's, 57
Winslow, Carleton M. (1877-1946), 227
Wiscasset, Maine, Nickels-Sortwell House, *24*
Withers, Frederick C. (1828-1901), 96
Withers and Vaux, 96
The Works in Architecture of Robert and James Adam, 29
Wotton, Sir Henry, 257
Wren, Sir Christopher (1632-1723), 13

"Wrenaissance," 167
Wright, Frank Lloyd (1867-1959), 131, 133, 195, 199, 200, 202-207, 238, 264-265, 267-268, 270, 272
Wright, Lloyd (b. 1890), 238
Wrightian, 263-268
Wurster, William W. (b. 1895), 212

Wyatt, James (1743-1813), 53, 56
Wyeth, Marion S. (b. 1889), 227

Yamasaki, Minoru (b. 1912), 257, 259-260, 262
Yeon, John, 212
Yonkers, New York, house near, 181
Young, Ammi B. (1800-1874), 41, 76, 77